When Jesus invites his followers to s[eek] after much more than a mere rearrang[ing] his intent is to give us a new way of see[ing] around which every part of life—family, work, friendship, money, leisure, power, play, and all the rest—must revolve. Few books do as good a job as this one in not only telling us, but *showing* us, how giving up everything for Christ and his kingdom is the pathway to God's greatest glory, the world's greatest cultivation and care, and our greatest gain. I highly commend Jeremy's work to you. *Seek First* is a gem.

Scott Sauls, senior pastor of Christ Presbyterian Church in Nashville, Tennessee, and author of *Befriend* and *Irresistible Faith.*

It's one of life's disorienting paradoxes: some of the most tormented souls are also some of the most successful. Long-term joy, fulfillment, and human flourishing can never be found in constructing our own kingdoms. So where is true joy and renewal found? In winsome ways, my friend Jeremy Treat shows us, by reminding us of another paradox. Yet this one is far more beautiful and fulfilling: it is when we put down our own kingdoms and seek first God's kingdom. *Seek First* is an inspiring reminder to keep first things first.

Bryan Loritts, author, *Insider Outsider*

If (like me) you've prayed "thy kingdom come" hundreds of times without really grasping the transformative scope of those words, then you need to read this book. With the same clarity, insight, and passion he exudes at the pulpit, Jeremy practically and powerfully reveals how—and more importantly, why—we ought to reorient our lives and reprioritize our loves around the one thing God tells us to seek above all else.

Marielle Wakim, deputy editor, *Los Angeles* magazine

In my day people searched for themselves by going to India, practicing Transcendental Meditation, or just going surfing. Today people surf the internet, search for themselves online, hire personal life coaches, and attend enrichment seminars in a never-ending quest for self-fulfillment. Jeremy Treat speaks a prophetic and urgent note to the generations: what matters most is seeking not yourself but the kingdom of God. *Seek First* is a clearly written and much-needed book that explains what Jesus meant by commanding his disciples to seek first the kingdom of God. Spoiler alert: it's not about doing one more thing but about inhabiting the framework that makes sense of and rightly orients everything else. Treat offers the best kind of life coaching: pastoral, theological direction for experiencing the reign of Jesus Christ in every aspect of our lives. Read this book, seek the kingdom, and discover the meaning of life.

Kevin J. Vanhoozer, research professor of systematic theology, Trinity Evangelical Divinity School

In *Seek First,* Jeremy Treat brings theology to the streets. He presents the message of the kingdom in a way that is both profound and practical, casting a grand vision for life and bringing majesty to the mundane, whether in the workplace or on the basketball court. I believe God will use this book to show people the tremendous joy, peace, and contentment that comes from seeking first the kingdom of God.

Chris Broussard, NBA analyst and sports broadcaster, founder and president of The K.I.N.G. Movement

Threading the kingdom story through the history of Israel and its fulfillment in Jesus Christ, Jeremy Treat deepens and widens our kingdom vision here and now. Reading this book, you'll want to stop and sing, "Rejoice, the Lord is king!"

Michael Horton, J. Gresham Machen Professor of Theology, Westminster Seminary California

With the theological vision of *The Crucified King*, it became clear Jeremy Treat is a first-rate theologian of the Word. In *Seek First* we see the fruit of years putting that vision to work at the heart of Los Angeles as a pastor-theologian of the church. With clear prose, careful theological and biblical exposition, vivid illustration, and relevant application, Jeremy invites regular Christians to focus on the one thing that really matters: the kingdom of God. Wide-ranging and surprisingly comprehensive, *Seek First* gives us an integrative vision of what it means to embrace, experience, and seek the kingdom of God in our everyday lives of work, play, service, and worship. Most importantly, he does this in every chapter by fixing our eyes firmly on the person and work of King Jesus, who is the kingdom in his very person. I really hope folks get their hands on this book.

Derek Rishmawy, PhD student at Trinity Evangelical Divinity School, columnist for *Christianity Today*, and cohost of the *Mere Fidelity* podcast

To explain something important, you usually must choose between being incisively passionate or comprehensively balanced. But this book chooses both and puts everything in its proper place. This is big-picture theology for everyone.

Fred Sanders, professor, Torrey Honors Institute, Biola University

Seek First is a wonderful gift that the extraordinary and innovative pastor Jeremy Treat has given the modern church. With this book, he reveals the concepts of God's kingdom along with how in practice God governs his people. As readers go through this book, they will come to know that God's kingdom is not a far, metaphysical, or futuristic phenomenon. They will firmly grasp that it is God's reign that is governing this land. Furthermore, Christians of all ages will know they are invited into the restoration of his kingdom and will receive a burning desire to serve the Lord. I recommend this book to all Christians who dream of our Father's kingdom.

Sanghoon Lee, professor, author, futurist for the Korean Missional Church Movement

Seek First is a work of love that is biblically solid and globally informed. The kingdom is not provincial but universal. Christian theology, therefore, ought to reflect the diversity of God's royal family. That is certainly the case for this book by Jeremy Treat. It is rooted in a particular social location and yet engages with global, theological, multiethnic voices simultaneously. It is a delightful experience to learn new names from around the world. Healthy family conversation with diverse past and present Christian theologies truly enriches the kingdom-of-God narrative. This evokes African wisdom known as *Ubuntu*: "I am, because we are."

Treat writes with clarity, beauty, and even poetry—reflecting a theology in the service of the mystery of the kingdom of God and the crucified and resurrected king. I shall remember the words of Jeremy Treat, a poet-theologian and pastor: "The cross is the throne from which the king of the world rules with grace." This is a book to reread, suited for contemplation and discussion.

Tekletsadik Belachew, researcher at Capuchin
Franciscan Research and Retreat Center in Addis Ababa,
Ethiopia, and PhD student in patristic history of exegesis,
Concordia Seminary

Before Jeremy Treat is a pastor who has written a book about the kingdom of God, he is a man who seeks to build his life around it. As someone who had the pleasure of working alongside Jeremy in Los Angeles for years, I got to see this first hand and benefit from his life. And that is what makes his writing so compelling. As a friend, I know that this book is not only the result of long hours poured out in reading and study (which it is) but also the fruit of learning to live it out in the community he leads in LA. In a restless and conflicted culture, *Seek First* is like a field guide for living life as Jesus intended.

Tim Chaddick, lead pastor, Reality Church London

SEEK FIRST

How the Kingdom of God Changes Everything

JEREMY TREAT

 ZONDERVAN®

ZONDERVAN

Seek First
Copyright © 2019 by Jeremy R. Treat

ISBN 978-0-310-58602-9 (softcover)

ISBN 978-0-310-58605-0 (audio)

ISBN 978-0-310-58603-6 (ebook)

Requests for information should be addressed to:
Zondervan, *3900 Sparks Dr. SE, Grand Rapids, Michigan 49546*

Some names and identifying details have been changed to protect the privacy of individuals.

Author represented by the literary agent Don Gates of The Gates Group, www .the-gates-group.com.

Cover design: Thinkpen Design
Cover illustration: Shutterstock
Interior design: Kait Lamphere

Printed in the United States of America

HB 03.04.2024

CONTENTS

ACKNOWLEDGMENTS

I dedicate this book to Mike Treat, who taught me the Scriptures as a kid, gave me pep talks before every basketball game growing up, and remains a constant model of humble confidence in my life today. Dad, you gave me everything that you never had, and for that I will forever be grateful. You've been through a lot in life, but you never gave up, you always kept fighting, and you've used everything God has given you to help others. For all these reasons and more, you're my hero.

To my wife, whose name is not on the cover of this book but whose fingerprints are all over it: Tiffany, you are God's greatest gift to me. Beyond being an incredible wife and mom, you are the kind of ministry partner who makes me so much better and brings joy to everything we do. I love you.

To my daughters, Ashlyn (8), Lauryn (7), Evelyn (5), and Katelyn (4): Every time I look at this book, I'll think of working on it with one of you sitting on my lap. I love you. I'm proud of you. And I pray that you always know God's love for you.

To my church family, Reality LA: My greatest joy in ministry (far more than writing books or speaking at conferences) is shepherding our church and preaching the word. Any ministry I do outside of the church flows from my role as your pastor. It is truly an honor to serve you, and I thank God that he's called me to be a part of our community in Los Angeles.

To the many friends, family, and mentors who have invested in me over the years: thank you. I am who I am, and this book is what it is, because of the many people who have taught me and cared for me. I'm grateful for my editors in this project, Ryan Pazdur and Chris Beetham, as well as Don Gates who has helped at every stage.

Lastly, and ultimately, all of this is for the glory of God. I'm a rebel who's been made a son and given a place at the king's table. All I can hope for is that my life amounts to an exhibit of God's royal grace. "Now to the King eternal, immortal, invisible, the only God, be honor and glory for ever and ever. Amen" (1 Tim 1:17).

Chapter 1

WHAT MATTERS
MOST

*Our greatest fear should not be of failure, but of succeeding at
something that doesn't really matter.*[1]

The key to life is finding out what matters most and building
your life around it. In an age of distraction, however, focusing
on what matters most feels impossible. Everything is grabbing
at our attention. Everyone is lobbying for our devotion. *Be this!
Do that! Give your life to my cause!*

It's not merely shallow or sinister temptations that pull us in
different directions. There are so many good things to keep up
with: friends, family, church, work, exercise, the news, and so on.
We end up feeling frantic, spread thin, and wondering if we're
even making a difference with our lives. An article in the *New
York Times* titled "The 'Busy' Trap" captures the tension well:

> Busyness serves as a kind of existential reassurance, a hedge
> against emptiness; obviously your life cannot possibly be
> silly or trivial or meaningless if you are so busy, completely
> booked, in demand every hour of the day. . . . I can't help but
> wonder whether all this histrionic exhaustion isn't a way of
> covering up the fact that most of what we do doesn't matter.[2]

So, what does matter? Sadly, we often confuse what's urgent with what's important and wear ourselves out by working on things that we won't be talking about in twenty years. Working hard is great. But it doesn't matter how hard we work if we are going in the wrong direction. We must be able to answer the question: *What matters most?*

You already have an answer to that question, even if you've never thought about it. If you want to know how your life answers that question, ask it this way instead: *What do I get most excited about? How do I use my time? Where do I spend my money?*

Or think about it another way: What are you building your life around? What's at the core that shapes the whole? Are you building your life around your career? Is it a relationship or a vision of family? Maybe it's what others think of you. In our culture, fame and success have become end goals without much substance (Successful at what? Famous for what?). If you focus more on being successful than on rightly defining success, then it won't matter whether you succeed or not.

We need to slow down to ponder what matters most and how it can give perspective to all the other important-but-not-ultimate things in our lives. The answer to life's deepest questions will not come from a secret place in your heart or from a *New York Times* journalist, or even from a pastor like myself. To understand what matters most, we need to look to the person who claimed to be the source of life and meaning itself, Jesus.

THE ONE THING JESUS COULDN'T STOP TALKING ABOUT

"What's the number one thing Jesus talked about?"—the preacher shouted in a classic you-should-know-this tone. Lucky for me, I was sure I knew the answer. After all, I had grown up in the church hearing every week about the love of God, the cross of

Christ, and the hope of spending eternity in heaven. As the preacher allowed a few seconds of silence to let the guilt build up for those who didn't know the answer, I smirked and prepared to mouth the words along with him. "The number one thing Jesus talked about was"—and then he said something that nearly knocked me off my pew—"the kingdom of God!"

The kingdom of God? I hardly knew anything about that. I'd heard sermons my whole life about faith in God, the forgiveness of sin, and being a part of the church. And Jesus talked more about the kingdom of God than all of those?

At that moment it was as if Conviction walked into the room and looked me in the eye; and then its friend Crisis came and sat next to me for an extended talk. How could I have spent a lifetime hearing about Jesus yet never studied or paid attention to the one thing Jesus talked about most? The kingdom had no place in my theology, my church life, or my perception of what it meant to be a Christian. That day was the beginning of a journey for me, a quest to understand the meaning of the kingdom of God, why it mattered so much to Jesus, and how it might affect my life.

In the weeks, months, and years that followed, I searched the Scriptures and became convinced the preacher was right. Jesus couldn't stop talking about the kingdom of God. When Jesus began his ministry, the first words out of his mouth were, "The time is fulfilled, and the kingdom of God is at hand; repent and believe in the gospel" (Mark 1:15). But this message of God's reign was not only the beginning of his ministry. Christ proclaimed the kingdom of God in his preaching and demonstrated it in his miracles and healings. Jesus was crucified as the king of the Jews (Matt. 27:37), he was raised from the dead as the king of the world (Eph. 1:20–23), and then he gathered his disciples to teach them for forty days about—guess what?—the kingdom of God (Acts 1:3).[3]

Jesus gave his followers many commands, but there was only one thing he said to seek *first*.

"Seek first the kingdom of God" (Matt. 6:33).

This is the one thing that changes everything. According to Jesus, what matters most in life is the kingdom of God.

IF THE KINGDOM MATTERS, EVERYTHING MATTERS

Jesus's command to "seek first the kingdom of God" wasn't shared in a classroom lecture or preached from a pulpit. Rather, Jesus was responding to his disciples' honest questions about the pressing needs of day-to-day life. They had left everything to follow Christ and now were wondering: *What will we eat? What should we wear? How can we balance all of life's needs?* Jesus reassured them, promising that if they would seek the kingdom of God before anything else in life, "all these things will be added to you" as well (Matt. 6:33). In other words, prioritizing the kingdom does not minimize the other aspects of life; it puts them in perspective.

The kingdom of God doesn't have to compete with our work, hobbies, relationships, and the other important aspects of life. In fact, when rightly understood, the kingdom will enhance every aspect of life, infusing them with fresh meaning and significance. As C. S. Lewis said, "When first things are put first, second things are not suppressed but increased."[4] What matters most gives perspective to anything that matters at all. Jesus spent so much time talking about the kingdom of God because it is not just another thing his disciples needed to learn. The kingdom of God was the framework for everything they needed to learn. "Seek first the kingdom" is a call to keep the main thing the main thing.

So let me ask you again: What is at the center of your life, exerting a gravitational pull to all your decisions and desires? If the dream or passion at the center of your life is something changing or temporary, not only will you constantly feel pulled in different directions, but you will always feel like you're one bad decision from falling part. The center cannot and will not hold. Only the kingdom of God is powerful enough to order and unite the various aspects of your life. That's why seeking first the kingdom is about more than setting priorities. The kingdom is not another thing on a long list of priorities; it is the framework determining the priorities. The kingdom of God, if you are willing to understand and embrace it, has the power to reorder your life with coherence and purpose.

WHAT IS THE KINGDOM OF GOD?

If the kingdom is so significant, then we ought to make sure we know what it means. While it will take this entire book to fully define what Jesus means by the "kingdom of God," it will help to have a working definition from the beginning. Let's start with this: *The kingdom is God's reign through God's people over God's place.*[5]

That's the message of the kingdom in eight words. Now let's break down each aspect to begin plumbing the depths of the kingdom of God.

God's Reign

The kingdom is first and foremost a statement about God. God *is* king, and he is coming *as* king to set right what our sin made wrong. The phrase "kingdom of God" could just as easily be translated "reign of God" or "kingship of God."[6] The message of the kingdom is about God's royal power directed by his self-giving love.

Claiming that the kingdom of God is primarily about *God* may seem obvious, but many today use "kingdom" to refer to the way *we* as human beings make the world a better place ("kingdom work") or to refer to all the Christians in the world ("kingdom minded"). Unfortunately, much of the contemporary talk about the kingdom paints a picture of a kingdom with a vacant throne. But if the kingdom is portrayed as a utopian world without

The Kingdom of God

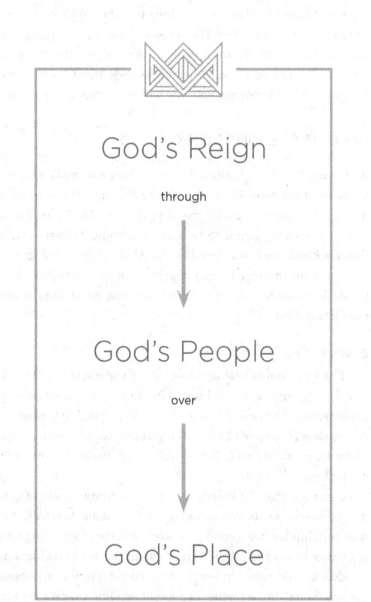

God's Reign

through

God's People

over

God's Place

mention of God, then the biblical idea of the kingdom has been lost. The kingdom of God is the vision of the world reordered around the powerful love of God in Christ.

God is king, and he reigns over his creation. But in a world marred by sin, God's kingship is resisted, and the peace of his kingdom has been shattered. After Adam and Eve's rebellion, God's reign is revealed as a redemptive reign. He is the king who is reclaiming his creation. The kingdom of God is not the culmination of human potential and effort but the intervention of God's royal grace into a sinful and broken world.

God's People

God the Creator-King reigns *over* all his creatures, but he also reigns *through* his people. This was God's design from the beginning. Adam and Eve were sent out from the garden as royal representatives of the king, called to steward his creation and spread the blessings of his reign throughout the earth. Instead, they chose to seek their own path to power and glory, apart from God. Their rebellion fractured humanity's relationship with God and shattered the goodness of his creation. Ever since sin entered the world, God's kingdom project has at its heart a rescue mission for rebellious sinners, drawing them into his work of renewing his creation as king.

God's reign is a saving reign. The kingdom of God provides a holistic understanding of salvation, including not only what we are saved *from*, but also what we are saved *for*:

We are saved *from* death and *for* life.
We are saved *from* shame and *for* glory.
We are saved *from* slavery and *for* freedom.
We are saved *from* sin and *for* following our savior.
We are saved *from* the kingdom of darkness and *for*
the kingdom of light.

To be saved into the kingdom of God is to have God's comprehensive rule over every aspect of life. This is a far cry from merely "asking Jesus into my heart." It means a new life, a new identity, and a new kingdom.

God's Place

The Bible is the story of God making his good creation a glorious kingdom. It all started in the garden, where God commissioned his people to go to the ends of the earth to make the rest of the world like Eden. The garden kingdom was meant to become a global kingdom where people would rejoice and the world would flourish under God's loving reign.

After the fall, making the world God's glorious kingdom would require a reversal of the curse and a renewal by grace. And that's exactly what God set out to do. The Bible is a rescue story, not about God rescuing sinners from a broken creation but about him rescuing them for a new creation. God's reign begins in the human heart, but it will one day extend to the ends of the earth. Many Christians today think of salvation as leaving earth for heaven, but the story of Scripture is quite the opposite. The message of the kingdom of God is not an escape from earth to heaven but God's reign coming from heaven to earth. The focus of God's reign is his people, but the scope of God's reign is all of creation.

Jesus and the Kingdom of God

This understanding of the kingdom of God may be new to you, but it would not have been surprising to the first-century crowds listening to Jesus. Their collective hope was that God would come as king to redeem his people and restore his creation. What surprised them about Jesus's proclamation was not *what* the kingdom is but *who* would bring it and *how* he would do so. Jesus fulfills every kingdom promise, but he establishes the kingdom in a way that is different than they expected and yet more glorious than they could have imagined. In our journey to understand the kingdom of God, this introduces a key element. The message of the kingdom is counterintuitive and surprising, going against the grain of worldly wisdom, because unlike any other kingdom this world has ever seen, Christ's kingdom is built on grace and advances with compassion. In this kingdom, the throne is a cross and the king reigns with self-giving love.[7]

GLIMPSES OF THE KINGDOM

My aim in this book is not only to help you understand the kingdom of God; I want you to experience it. The *message* of the kingdom will awaken your mind and stir your affections, but the *power* of the kingdom will change your life. I write with my Bible open and aim to tell the story faithfully. But I also write with an open heart, as a man who believes in the power of the kingdom because I have been transformed by it. And not just me—God's kingdom is bringing renewal in people, communities, and cities throughout the world. Hearing some of these stories will not only give a glimpse of the kingdom but also invite us to live in light of the king.

The Kingdom in Nairobi

Several years ago, I visited Nairobi, Kenya. The memories of the wildlife, the landscape, and the beautiful people of Kenya will always be with me. Yet the most vivid memories are of my visit to the slums of Kibera. When I first learned that we were going to a "slum," I pictured an impoverished alley with a handful of people in it. But nothing prepared me for what I saw when I stepped out of the car. This "slum" stretched as far as my eyes could see. Over one million people call Kibera "home."

We entered the slum and followed an open stream of sewage that carved a path through the shelters made of scrap wood and mud. Children ran around without clothes and played in the mud. An empty Sprite bottle glistened in the sun as it floated down the stream of sewage. As we passed a young girl sitting on the side of the path, a local man whispered in my ear that she was a prostitute, used by the men in the village for only a quarter.

She was twelve years old.

Overwhelmed by the brokenness surrounding me, I heard a faint noise in the distance. I couldn't tell what it was, but I knew it was worth paying attention to. We kept walking, and the noise grew louder and louder. It was a rumbling, indistinct sound. As we got closer, it became apparent that it was the sound of people. Were they yelling? Shouting? Chanting?

My thoughts were interrupted by an opening in the path. Directly in front of us was a small building; little more than a shack. Suddenly I realized what the noise was: the sound of many voices joined together in song.

As soon as we stepped inside the shack, I knew exactly where we were. It was a church service. Sixty to seventy people filled a space not much larger than my living room. They were all singing at the top of their lungs, praising God in Swahili. A woman's uplifted arms were so thin and frail that I could see the shape of her bones, yet those arms were raised high toward heaven in worship.

Tears. Smiles. Prayer. Praise. I sat for several minutes, taking it all in, and my soul was convicted and comforted in a way that has had a lasting impact on me. Why? Because in that impoverished slum, I knew that the kingdom had come. It had not yet arrived in the fullness of God's future promise, but it was there, in the midst of the most horrific suffering and brokenness I've seen. It was a snapshot of the message that Jesus announced and the reason I am writing this book: God's reign was breaking in and transforming the lives of real people. These people had nothing, yet they knew that in Christ they had everything. God's reign was present to them, and they received it with joy. God's love was poured out on them, and it flowed outward through them. Throughout the day, I heard stories of how these people loved and served others in their community. What I saw in that little shack was a glimpse of the same power that will one day renew all of creation.

The Kingdom in Los Angeles

On another occasion I sat in a very different context but saw evidence of the same powerful grace. I leaned back in my chair at an artisan coffee shop on Sunset Boulevard, sipping my pour-over coffee and listening with intent. The man across the table had tattoos covering every inch of his arms and a look on his face that expressed the kind of joy that comes only on the other side of hard times.

Years earlier Jaden had dedicated his life to building his own kingdom and making a name for himself. He was good at it too. He had achieved what most people dream of (but few realize) when they come to Los Angeles.

"When I got everything I had always wanted, I realized that it wasn't what I wanted," he said to me. When Jaden hit a low point, he remembered a coworker mentioning our church—literally in a conversation where Jaden was making fun of his friend for being "so religious." He never expected when he walked into the high school auditorium that morning that he would leave an entirely different person. When Jaden heard the gospel for the first time, he trusted in Christ as king and immediately experienced the newness of life with God. "It's not that I found God. He found me, and his grace melted away the hardness of my heart." Jaden sensed something beautiful happening inside him and knew that it would touch every aspect of his world. The entire trajectory of his life had been forever changed.

Here again, as I sat and listened to his story, I knew that the kingdom of God had come. God's gracious reign had overcome his resistant heart. That day he became a child of the king.

Not only did he know God, but he was drawn into God's mission. Since that day when he met Jesus, Jaden has led many people to the Lord. He has experienced God's grace in his own life, and he has seen it flow through him to others. The places where he lives, works, and plays have become territory for his king.

The Kingdom in Galilee

The day began like any other, the same old routine of sitting by the road begging for handouts. This Middle-Eastern man couldn't see or speak, and he was tormented by demons. In addition to his physical suffering, he endured social shame and the isolation that comes with being an outcast. But this day would be different. Some people passing by had sympathy for the man and led him to a visiting miracle worker who was healing people. Blind and mute, the man heard a powerful yet gentle voice speaking in Aramaic with a Galilean accent. Moments later he opened his eyes for the first time. Looking up, he saw the face of Jesus.

When the crowd saw what had happened, they immediately wondered—who is this miracle worker? Could he be the promised king, the Messiah? Their awe, however, quickly turned into an argument, debating among themselves where such power could come from. Their conclusion, as strange as it sounds, was that it must be the power of the devil.

Jesus would have none of that nonsense. His words pierced through the chaos, boldly declaring the source and significance of his healing power: "If it is by the Spirit of God that I cast out demons, then the kingdom of God has come upon you" (Matt. 12:28). This was not the work of the devil or the product of human ingenuity but an invasion of God's power, a clash of kingdoms. The royal power of God had broken into a world marred by sin, bringing renewal and restoration. And by his words and actions, Jesus was also making a statement about his identity. The kingdom of God had arrived through the Son of God.

An Everyday Kingdom

My hope is that you would have kingdom stories of your own to tell. The kingdom of God is more than a theological concept or a distant reality. We experience the kingdom whenever and wherever God's redemptive reign overcomes our sinful resistance. It is present in the daily challenges and joys of life, as well as those miraculous moments that leave us awestruck. And the evidence of God's kingdom is that it brings transformation to all of life, including the mundane.

My life is, for the most part, pretty normal. I go to work at 8:00 a.m., have dinner with my family every night at 5:30 p.m., and try to stay out of the news. And yet I see God's reign breaking in and bringing renewal and restoration in more ways than I could count. Heaven is breaking in during our family conversations at the dinner table. Heaven is breaking in as I talk with my neighbors in the front yard. Heaven is breaking in through the text messages I send to the group of men I meet with who have committed to pray for one another. Heaven is breaking in during the gloriously mundane routine of gathering each week with the body of Christ on Sundays. The message of the kingdom is powerful and practical. It is supernatural, yet it often appears in surprisingly ordinary ways.

REARRANGING LIFE AROUND WHAT MATTERS MOST

My aim is to help you learn how to rearrange your life around what matters most. This won't come naturally. It won't be easy. You'll need to resist some of your habits and work against your normal tendencies. But it's worth it. To experience the life Jesus says we were made for, we need to have kingdom perspective, live with kingdom purpose, and learn to be kingdom people. This is the beginning of a journey.

In the first part of the book, we'll gain perspective on what the kingdom of God is and how it shapes all of life. In chapter 2 we'll see how the kingdom can only be understood through the grand narrative of Scripture. This is not just a story of what happened in Bible times, it is the story that continues to make sense of our lives today. Chapter 3 will bring clarity on the kingdom by introducing us to the king himself, Jesus. Christ's life, death, and resurrection are the key to understanding the kingdom of God. In chapter 4 we'll see that putting the kingdom first clarifies and enhances every other aspect of life. A robust vision of God's reign over all creation has profound implications for the way we think about work, rest, play, food, and art.

Once we've gained a kingdom perspective on life, we're called to live it out with purpose. This is the focus of part 2 of the book. Chapter 5 looks at the call to follow the king and how that creates a path of growth and maturity. Chapter 6 talks about the community of the king, the church. The church is not the same as the kingdom, but it serves as a preview, an outpost, and an instrument of the kingdom today. Chapter 7 describes how justice is an essential aspect of the kingdom and how the king's people are called to do justice, love kindness, and walk humbly with God (Mic. 6:8).

Living with kingdom perspective and being driven by a kingdom purpose requires a shift in our identity as well. So the third part of the book discusses our identity as kingdom people. Chapter 8 looks at how we are sons and daughters of the king, commissioned to live in light of our royal resemblance. Chapter 9 teaches that we are sojourners and exiles who are called to faithfulness to the kingdom as we follow Christ in a land that is not yet our home. We are dual citizens, but our allegiance to God's kingdom takes priority over and shapes our responsibility to the city of man. Chapter 10 acknowledges the tension we feel in this life as saints and sinners. The kingdom has already come, but it has not yet come in fullness. In between the "already" and "not yet" of the kingdom we are called to live with power for today and hope for tomorrow.

This book is an invitation to stop building our own personal kingdoms and start living for the one thing that matters most—the kingdom of God. The Croatian theologian Miroslav Volf offers a solemn warning: "The main temptation is not to reject God outright, but to embrace God as something secondary and use God as an instrument for our own ends."[8] The only way to avoid our tendency to use God for our purposes is to acknowledge God as king and build our lives around his kingdom.

KINGDOM PERSPECTIVE

Chapter 2

A MASTER
NARRATIVE

The way we understand human life depends on this question:
What is the real story of which my life story is part?

Lesslie Newbigin, *The Gospel*
in a Pluralist Society

I love stories, and I love going to the place where there are
more stories per square inch than anywhere: the bookstore.
I will never forget one trip in particular. I was doing my usual
thing—perusing the books, aimlessly looking for something
that might catch my eye—when I randomly pulled out a book
titled *The Artist of the Beautiful* by J. D. Landis. I had never
heard of the author, nor of this book, but the title intrigued
me, so I pulled it off the shelf and read the description on the
back cover.

The fate of Swift River Valley holds a strange fascination for
seventeen-year-old Sarianna Renway, a wayward student
obsessed with the life and work of poet Emily Dickinson.
In the small hamlet of Greenwich Village—abandoned,
beautiful, doomed—Sarianna takes a job tutoring a
minister's son.

Honestly, I wasn't interested. It was disappointing. But as I leaned in to set the book back on the shelf, I happened to read the next sentence in the description.

A man of deep faith, Jeremy Treat strives to instill hope into a town destined to be taken and lost forever.[1]

"What! Jeremy Treat? That's me! *I'm* Jeremy Treat." I looked around in shock, wondering if someone was playing a joke on me. And just like that, I was hooked. What had looked boring a moment before now had me entranced. Why? Now, it was personal. A story comes alive when you find your place within it.

There is another book that has had the same effect on millions of people over thousands of years. You may not find your name written in it, but you'll find your story. Because not only is the Bible the greatest story ever told, it is *the* story that makes sense of our lives.

THE POWER OF NARRATIVE

Whether sitting around a campfire, listening to a song, or watching a movie, we have all been captivated by the tension of an unfolding plot. Stories not only fascinate us, they also shape us. When I was a kid, I would watch the same movies over and over again so many times that I would start to see my own life through that narrative. My problems were kryptonite, my enemies were Lex Luthor, and my bedroom was a phone booth that would transform me into Superman. The stories we hear shape the way we view the world and ourselves.

Stories are not just for children, stimulating our imaginations until we grow up and live in the real world of logic and reason. Stories produce meaning in our lives. Bare facts are helpful, but they only find coherence and have significance when they are placed within a broader narrative.

IN SEARCH OF A MASTER NARRATIVE

We all live according to stories. But it's not the small stories that shape us most. We all long to see our lives as part of a bigger story. We are in search of a master narrative, a comprehensive story that answers the big questions of life.

Why are we here?
What's wrong?
What's the remedy?
How will it end?

A master narrative is the story that frames your life and the lens through which you see the world. Take the American Dream, for example. More than just an idea, the American Dream is a controlling story that shapes the way many (even some living outside of America) think and live. The narrative of the American Dream answers all the questions of life. Why are we here? The pursuit of happiness. What's wrong? We haven't yet experienced the fullness of security, safety, and freedom. What's the remedy? We are—good, hardworking people who defy limits and create our destinies. How will it end? With a white picket fence, 2.3 kids, and a backyard so we can enjoy life without having to interact with our neighbors.

Few people would admit that they live by the narrative of the American Dream (or any other master narrative, for that matter). This is because master narratives are usually assumed rather than explicitly acknowledged. The stories we live by are less about what we consciously believe and more about what we take for granted. A master narrative is usually revealed by what is unquestioned or common sense in a culture.

For example, consider the common phrase, "Be true to yourself." In American culture this advice comes across as virtuous wisdom. Being true to yourself, however, only makes sense in a hyper-individualistic society that lives within a larger narrative of self-fulfillment. If someone said, "Be true to yourself," in a culture that values the community before the individual (which describes most cultures throughout the history of the world), the listener would be confused. "Why wouldn't I be true to my family? Or my community?" In an individualistic culture, being "true to yourself" feels like commonsense wisdom. But that's only because it's heard in the context of a broader plotline that glorifies autonomy and culminates in personal satisfaction.

COMPETING NARRATIVES

We all live according to a master narrative, whether we know it or not. But there are a variety of cultural narratives on the market, and there is competition for which of them will shape your life. Secular narratives tell the story of the world as emerging from the Dark Ages of religious fairy tales to enter the light of human potential and progress.[2] Many religious narratives are about souls escaping the corrupted material world for the bliss of an eternal spiritual existence. In the Western world, you'll find a deep baseline narrative that is often held by religious and irreligious people alike. The functional master narrative of most people in Western cultures is one that places the sovereign self at the center of the universe and culminates in individual happiness. Our lives are defined by a story that is about "finding myself," "following my heart," and discovering "my best life."

Here is the frightening part: *it is possible to have Christian beliefs yet still live by another narrative.* We can say we hold to the Christian doctrines of the inspiration of Scripture, the deity of Christ, and justification by faith. We can identify as a Christian and go to church on Sundays. Yet in our day-to-day lives we may still be living by a secular narrative that is about building our own kingdoms.

Take Rob, for example. Rob grew up in the church, believed the key tenets of the faith, and avoided the "major sins" in the Bible. Rob came to see me one day, wanting to know why God had let him down. Rob had done everything right but was not experiencing success in the career he believed God had called him to and hadn't met the Christian woman he'd been praying for all these years. Rob felt like he'd done his part and was left wondering, "Why isn't God doing his part?"

Have you ever felt that way? What's really going on here? Did God actually let Rob down? I think Rob had been hijacked by a different narrative, a secularized version of the American Dream that promised fame for hard work and material blessing for spiritual focus. And he'd learned to reconcile this alternative narrative with his Christian faith by calling his career a "platform" for God. He had unrealistic expectations for a wife: the "Proverbs 31 woman" who looks like the girl on the cover of a magazine and won't ask him to change. Rob was in a place many Christians in America find themselves today: mad at God for breaking promises that he never made.

Sadly, I believe many Christians today have been hijacked by a cultural narrative, and even worse, have learned how to baptize it with Christian lingo. In response, we need more than right beliefs with a bit of morality mixed in. We need a more compelling narrative, and that's exactly what Jesus gives us in the story of the kingdom of God.

THE GRANDEST STORY OF ALL

While many Christians are familiar with the individual stories of the Bible—Noah's ark, David and Goliath, Jesus walking on water—fewer know how these stories connect and fit together. Scripture is not a mismatch of stories about morality; it is one grand story of God's royal grace.[3] And Jesus tells the story of the Bible as a kingdom story. "The time is *fulfilled*, the kingdom of God is at hand" (Mark 1:15). This is the language of plot and resolution. When Jesus spoke of the kingdom of God, he was not simply discussing a doctrine; he was evoking an entire story. It's the story of God making his broken creation into a beautiful kingdom. This story unfolds with twists and turns, sorrow and joy—it's the greatest plot in the history of literature—and climaxes with God's loving reign, a people flourishing, and the earth rejoicing.

The story of the kingdom of God is the master narrative for the people of God. It answers the big questions of life and gives a lens through which to see the world.

Big Questions of Life	The Kingdom Story
Why Are We Here?	The kingdom project
What's Wrong?	Rebellion against the king
What's the Remedy?	Promise of the kingdom (Israel) Coming of the kingdom (Christ)
How Will It End?	The eternal kingdom

The Kingdom Project

Why am I here? What is the purpose of life? The opening pages of the Bible answer these questions by showing God's intention for the world. God created the earth out of nothing, and his plan was for it to be a glorious kingdom where all that he made would flourish under his loving reign. The first chapters of the Bible reveal the pattern for the kingdom: God's reign through God's people over God's place.

Genesis 1–2 portrays God as sovereign Creator, the maker of

heaven and earth, whose act of creation establishes his rule over all he has made. Like most kings, God rules through his word. He speaks, and it happens. "Let there be light," he said, and there was light.

Many people today, especially those of us in the United States, have not lived under a monarchial government, and the idea of a king feels foreign. "The king" may conjure up thoughts of Elvis Presley, Michael Jackson, or LeBron James. But these figures, although very skilled in their own domain, are a far cry from the ancient understanding of a monarch.

Our understanding of kingship has also been tarnished by rulers throughout history who have used fear, violence, and oppression to enforce their rule. Ivan the Terrible, for example, was a Russian ruler known for his cruelty and irrational outbursts. He built a wall around his city so that no one could escape and had his troops gather up to one thousand people a day to be tortured and killed right in front of him and his son. Many kings have ruled through fear and used their power for wicked purposes.

God is a different type of king, a *good* king. He rules with wisdom, justice, mercy, and self-giving love. God is as patient as he is powerful. He is as beautiful as he is strong. He is as merciful as he is mighty. He's a good king. God's power is guided by his love and is always in line with his character. He is the kind of king who uses his power to bless his people.

After speaking creation into existence, what God did next was shocking. The king stooped down, got his hands dirty, and created humanity from the dust, like a potter forming clay with gentleness and precision. The power of the king's word was matched only by the care of his hands. God is the maker of all things, but humanity—and only humanity—is made in the "image of God" (Gen. 1:26–28). God's people are the crown of his creation.

God placed his people in the garden of Eden and said to them, "You may surely eat of every tree of the garden, but of the tree of the knowledge of good and evil you shall not eat" (Gen. 2:16–17). Unfortunately, many have focused so much on the prohibition of the one fruit that they have overlooked the invitation to feast on all the other fruits. The God who abounds in love and kindness created a world of delights and placed his beloved image bearers in it with an invitation to enjoy.

God is for our joy. He's not a cosmic killjoy who makes life difficult so that he can watch us suffer. Taste buds were God's idea. Sex was God's idea. Pleasure was God's idea. Adam and Eve had the freedom to eat, play, rest, and delight in the goodness of God's creation. And to be clear: this was not just a spiritual joy, detached from the material world. "God saw everything that he had made, and behold, it was very good" (Gen. 1:31). The garden represented the goodness of the spiritual and material, the personal and social, and all of it was for our good and God's glory.

God was for Adam's joy, but when he placed him in the garden, he did not give him a vacation. God gave him a task. Genesis 2:15 says, "The LORD God took the man and put him in the garden of Eden to work it and keep it." God entrusted to humanity something very important to him. This was a call to responsible stewardship.

God placed Adam and Eve in the garden of Eden and called them to care for it, but he also called them to expand its borders to the ends of the earth. Eden was a beautiful garden with order and harmony, while the rest of the world was wild and untamed. The world was good, but it was created with potential, full of resources that needed to be cultivated. Genesis 1–2 presents us not with a final product, but with an unfinished project. Adam and Eve were called to Edenize the world.

Immediately after making humanity in his image, God gave them a mandate: "Be fruitful and multiply and fill the earth and *subdue it*, and have *dominion* . . . over every living thing that moves on the earth" (Gen. 1:28). This is royal language. *Subdue* the earth. Have *dominion* over it. Humans are made to be sub-rulers on God's behalf, sons and daughters of the king who represent their Father's benevolent reign.[4] To rule over the earth means not to exploit creation or abuse its resources, but quite the opposite: to care for and cultivate God's creation as stewards who have been entrusted with something precious to God. To be image bearers of God means to be sent out as ambassadors, representing the king and his kingdom.

This is not how most people think of Eden. The common assumption is that God created the world perfect and complete, sin marred God's perfect creation, and so the goal of redemption is to get back to Eden. This is partially correct, but doesn't go far enough. Salvation is aimed at recovering Eden *and* the Edenic vision of God's reign over all the earth. The kingdom is about God's reign over every nook and cranny of this planet. As the Indian theologian Ken Gnanakan says, "God has an ultimate plan for his world and that . . . plan relates to his kingdom."[5]

Rebellion against the King

Everyone knows that something is wrong with the world. The joy and flourishing that we were made for has been tainted by the pain and brokenness that we experience in our lives. What went wrong?

As quickly as a snake can slither into a garden, an alternative narrative was introduced into God's world.

> Did God actually say, "You shall not eat of any tree in the garden"? (Gen. 3:1)

The serpent, who is later revealed to be the devil, questioned God's character by twisting God's word. The enemy seeks to steal, kill, and destroy. But don't be fooled. This warrior comes not with tanks and bombs but with cunning questions, half-truths, and masked lies. The devil could not force Adam and Eve to sin. His power is in deception and his influence is in allure. He takes something destructive and makes it look beautiful.

The temptation in Eden was not about eating fruit; it was about exercising autonomy. *Why be ruled by God when you can rule yourself?* And with a bite, the trajectory of human history was changed forever. While the juice was still dripping from Eve's chin, the corruption of Adam and Eve's wayward hearts began spreading throughout the goodness of God's creation.

What Adam and Eve did is what the Bible calls "sin." Many people associate sin with God forbidding us from enjoying the good things in life, a way of testing us to see if we are really committed to him. But as we've learned, God is for our good. His rules are not prohibitions of fun; they are boundaries for freedom. More than just breaking rules, sin is rebellion against the ruler.

A throne never remains empty. Sin is not only *rebellion* against God, it is a *replacement* of God. We were made to find satisfaction, meaning, and security in God. When we look for those things in money, fame, sex, or career, it's a slap in the face to our Maker. It's a declaration that we want all that God provides but that we don't want God himself. The Bible refers to these God replacements as idols. An idol is anything you worship or live for in place of God. It is whatever sits on the throne of your heart, ruling your life and directing your desires, dreams, and decisions.

We're all ruled by something. Many people are ruled by their careers. They worship success, sacrifice their family and friends, and serve their employers. For others, having the right physical appearance rules their life. They worship at the altar of bodily perfection, sacrifice their time and money to achieve the perfect look, and wait vigilantly to be noticed and adored. Countless idols fill the marketplace of human desire: the yearning for approval, the longing for security, the craving of fame, the possessing of wealth. But do not be deceived. Anything that rules over you other than God will be a harsh king. It will make promises that it cannot keep. It will disappoint you and then blame you, telling you it's all your fault. Whatever you look to in order to satisfy you will end up enslaving you. The reign of God brings freedom; the reign of everything else leads to slavery.

The nature of sin penetrates deeper still. If I am the one who picks and chooses the idols I serve and decides what is right and wrong, then the ultimate object of my worship and devotion is not the idols of money, sex, or power—it is self. Sin is our attempt to dethrone God and enthrone ourselves. While humanity was made to live for *God's* kingdom and glorify *his* name, sin is our attempt to build our own kingdom and make a name for ourselves. Sin is *autonomy*, a word, which when broken into its component parts, means "self-rule." Sin is the attempt to dethrone God and replace him with the sovereign self, where individual desire reigns, personal choice is our authority, and freedom is defined by independence.

The irony is that in all our attempts to rule ourselves, we end up submitting to the rule of another, the serpent king who deceived our parents in Eden. The deception of autonomy was his plan all along: to allure us with self-rule so that in thinking we run our own lives, we increase in our rebellion against the good and holy king.

From the garden a rival kingdom emerged. Adam and Eve were originally sent out to spread the blessings of God's kingdom throughout the world, but instead they were banished and ended up spreading the curse of human sin to the ends of the earth. When God's reign is received, it is experienced as grace. When God's reign is resisted, it is experienced as judgment.

THE PROMISE OF A SERPENT-CRUSHING KING

Everyone agrees that something is wrong with the world, but there are never-ending opinions when it comes to the solution. According to the Scriptures, the starting place is not human potential, technological advancement, or more education. It is grace. By an act of undeserved favor, God set out to reverse the curse of humanity's sin and restore the blessings of his reign. He would not give up on his kingdom project.

In Genesis 3:15, against the backdrop of God's judgment of Adam and Eve and the curse of the serpent, a ray of hope shined forth. The Lord declared that while there would be enmity between humanity and the serpent, a descendent of a woman would one day crush the head of the serpent, although this victor would be wounded in the process. This was a seed planted in Eden that would grow throughout the rest of the biblical story: the promise of a serpent-crushing king who would rescue God's people and renew God's creation.[6] Sin had hardened the hearts of God's people and the soil of God's creation. But, to borrow from the poetry of Tupac Shakur, a rose began to emerge through a crack in the concrete.[7]

God's purposes prevail: He would reign over his creation as king with his people enjoying the blessings of his kingdom. The presence of sin, however, meant that there must be a new route to this goal. Genesis 3:15 shows the way, revealing that the promise of victory would include the price of suffering. A pattern emerges in the story of Scripture from this point onward: victory comes through suffering, exaltation through humiliation, and ultimately, the kingdom through the cross. The light that would one day shine on the cross of Christ casts a shadow all the way back to this great promise. The ruin of humanity's sin will be overcome by the reign of humanity's Savior.

The rest of the Bible is the story of God keeping this promise of a sacrificial, serpent-crushing king. Through the unfolding plot of the Old Testament, we begin to see how God's reign through God's people over God's place will bring renewal in a world marred by sin.

A pivotal moment in God's mission would involve a man who would become known as Abraham. God did not choose Abraham because he was superspiritual, as if he won a *Mesopotamian Idol* contest and earned his way into God's plan. In truth, Abraham was a moon-worshiping pagan from the land of Babel, the very place where human sin culminated in the attempt to build a tower to reach heaven by human effort. Instead, God chose Abraham by grace. The Bible is not the story of God finding good people and rewarding them; it's the story of God pursuing wicked people and saving them. God made a threefold promise to Abraham (Gen. 12:1–3):

1. To make his descendants a great people
2. To give them a place, the promised land
3. Through him to bless all the families of the earth

Echoes of Eden abound: a people, a place, and a plan to bring the blessings of God's reign to the ends of the earth.

After God's declaration of a serpent-crushing king and his promise of people, land, and blessing to Abraham, God initiated a covenant. This covenant is key because it is the means by which God's kingdom is realized throughout the story line of the Old Testament.

What is a covenant? If you've ever had a DTR ("define the relationship" conversation), you can understand a bit of what's going on here. If you aren't familiar with a DTR, it's what happens in a relationship when you move from "hello" to "we're a thing." At some point, in every relationship that has a hope of lasting, you have to sit down and define the relationship: *Are we dating, seeing each other, boyfriend and girlfriend?* When God initiates a covenant, he's having a DTR with his people. He is defining the relationship. A covenant is a binding agreement based on vows that create a new relationship, making those involved as close as family. That's how we use the word when we talk about a marriage (a covenant relationship), and that's how God uses the word with his people. He binds himself by grace to his people. As the Old Testament story progressed, God's kingdom came through a series of covenants, each different but related.

God's covenant people multiplied, quickly fulfilling God's promise to Abraham to make his people as numerous as the sand on the seashore (Gen. 22:17). These people would eventually become known as the nation of Israel, God's chosen people. But they were not chosen to the exclusion of the rest of the world. On the contrary, Israel was chosen as God's vehicle to reach the rest of the world, as the fulfilment of God's promise to bless all the families of the earth (Gen. 12:3).

God's redemptive reign had created a *people*, but they were in the wrong *place*. So God redeemed his people out of slavery in Egypt and set them on their way toward the promised land. What should have been a short journey turned into forty years of wandering in the wilderness. Eventually God's people entered into the promised land under the leadership of Joshua and settled into the land under the kingship of Saul, David, and then Solomon. But even though Israel was numerous, living in the promised land, and living under a God-appointed king, the root of the problem—human sin and rebellion—remained. God's grace was repeatedly met with hearts hardened by sin. And just as Adam and Eve sinned against God and were banished from Eden, Israel chose their own way and were exiled from the promised land. The Old Testament ends with a defeated people longing for the serpent-crushing king who could fulfill God's kingdom purposes.

The Coming of the Kingdom through Christ

In most cultural narratives, the problem is "out there" and we are the answer. In the story of Scripture, we are the problem and Jesus is the answer. But Jesus is not a generic superhero. He's the Messiah, Israel's long-awaited Savior who would fulfill all of God's promises: a reconciled people, a renewed place, and all flourishing under God's reign.

When Jesus arrived on the scene, he not only proclaimed the kingdom, he embodied it. Christ is a picture of God's kingdom in a person. Jesus's perfect life, however, is not enough to bring the kingdom of God. An example to follow is insufficient to save us from slavery to sin. We need a savior: a king who lives a righteous life and has the power to redeem us from our unrighteous lives.

This is what Jesus accomplished through his death and resurrection. The cross is Christ's throne from which he reigns with self-giving love. The essence of sin is our attempt to take God's place on the throne. The essence of salvation is God taking our place on the cross. When Jesus rose from the grave, it was a public declaration that nothing could stop God's reign from advancing on earth, not even death. Jesus is the resurrected king who brings God's mercy and majesty to a world marred by sin.

Through the gospel, God not only draws people to himself, but he draws us into his kingdom mission. Jesus, after he ascended into heaven, sent the Holy Spirit to continue his work in and through the church as the community of the kingdom. Wherever God's reign breaks in and is received with faith, there is the kingdom of God. God's reign is advancing amid the very brokenness of our world.

The Eternal Kingdom

The kingdom has already come in Christ but will not yet be fully realized until Christ's return. In between the already and not yet of the kingdom of God, Jesus calls his people to his mission.

The church is the signpost and foretaste of the kingdom of God, advancing God's kingdom purposes and giving the world a sneak preview of the future. God advances his kingdom through the church, as his people are conformed day by day to the image of Christ, even in his suffering. One day the story will reach a complete resolution. When Jesus returns as king, he will renew all things—ridding the world of evil, reconciling his people, and renewing his creation—finally and ultimately making the world God's kingdom.

The final chapter of the biblical story is not a disembodied heaven with harp-playing souls floating on clouds. The goal is heaven and earth coming together—a new creation. This is why the Bible ends with a picture of Jesus on the throne, proclaiming, "Behold, I am making all things new" (Rev. 21:5). Eternity is Christ reigning over and through redeemed people from every tribe and people and language and nation in a world renewed by grace.[8]

FINDING YOUR PLACE IN THE STORY

A story grabs you when you find your place in it. Jesus is inviting us to find our place in his kingdom story. The Bible is not a collection of moral stories that we imitate through works; it is a royal story of grace that we get swept into by faith. It's the master narrative that brings coherence and meaning to our lives.

Chapter 3

AN UNMATCHABLE
KING

Alexander, Caesar, Charlemagne, and I have founded empires. But on what did we rest the creations of our genius? Upon force. Jesus Christ founded his empire upon love; and at this hour millions of men would die for him. Napoleon Bonaparte[1]

In 1934, as the world was trembling under the threat of global war, the people of Hungary were swept into German influence and declared war on the United States. A telegraph relates one of the exchanges from that time:

"Hungary, Hungary, are you a republic?"
"No sir, we are a kingdom."
"Really? Who is your king?"
"We don't have a king. . . ."
"Curious, a kingdom without a king . . ."[2]

The kingdom of the Hungarian people didn't last long. In the following years, it fell apart due to a lack of leadership and unity. What else would you expect of a kingdom without a king?

Sadly, many Christians today are promoting what amounts to a kingdom without a king. People talk about "kingdom justice" or "kingdom living," in a way that eclipses the person and work of Christ the king. For some, "kingdom work" seems to be no different than a secular attempt to make the world a better place.[3] This approach couldn't be further from the truth. To genuinely embrace the kingdom, we have to keep the focus on Jesus the king.

But there's a problem: there are many versions of Jesus out there.

IN SEARCH OF THE REAL JESUS

The panoply of Jesuses is not a new problem. The apostle Paul, only twenty years or so after Jesus's resurrection, reported that already several versions of Jesus existed (2 Cor. 11:4). Throughout history this problem has perpetuated as people have attempted to make Jesus into their own image. Here are a few of the more common portraits of Jesus in Western culture today.

Jesus as Cosmic Vending Machine

Many people come to Jesus as if he were a cosmic vending machine. If you pay your dues (through church attendance, Bible reading, or using replacement swear words), Jesus is supposed to give you whatever you want. The problem here is that you're not following or worshiping Jesus; you're using him for your own purposes. This Jesus dispenses stuff, whereas the biblical Jesus calls us to himself.

Jesus as Divine Cheerleader

The divine cheerleader Jesus is always there when you are having a rough day. He helps you discover your potential and gives encouragement so you can achieve your best life. This Jesus exists to pat you on the back and say you're okay. But the divine cheerleader Jesus ignores sin and therefore the need for being saved. This Jesus has pom-poms in his hands rather than nails.

Jesus as Heavenly Firefighter

Some see Jesus as a heavenly firefighter to call on when in need of help. This Jesus exists to rescue you from trouble so you can get back to leading your own life. He's there for emergencies, but *only* for emergencies. The problem with firefighter Jesus is that you don't really know him, you just use him. He's not looked to as a savior as much as a backup plan for disasters.

JESUS, THE KING OF THE KINGDOM

The real Jesus is not a vending machine, a cheerleader, or a firefighter. The Jesus of the Bible is a king, a loving and gracious king. That's why Jesus is called the "Christ." We refer to him as "Jesus Christ," but I like to remind people that "Christ" is not Jesus's last name. Nobody called him "Mr. Christ," and if he had a jersey it wouldn't have said "Christ" on the back. "Christ" is a title that means *messiah*, which refers to his position as the promised savior king of Israel.[4]

Jesus is not the kind of king who sits back on his throne, arms folded, waiting for us to get our act together. He rules actively. He initiates. He pursues. He loves. That's why Jesus came proclaiming "the gospel of the kingdom" (Matt. 24:14). The word *gospel* literally means "good news." The kingdom of God is good news because the king reigns with grace. Most kings would destroy those who rebel against them. Jesus invites us into his family and gives us a place at his table. The essential message of the kingdom of God is not good advice about what you need to do to clean up your act and win God's approval. It's good news about what God has done for us in Christ.[5]

The gospel is what makes the Christianity unique. Most religions are about ascending to God through works. The Christian faith is about God descending to us in grace. That's good news. And all this good news is centered on Jesus. The minute we turn the kingdom into a human-effort project, we lose its very nature. It's the kingdom *of God*. It is a kingdom of grace. As Lesslie Newbigin said, "When the message of the kingdom is divorced from the person of Jesus, it becomes a programme or an ideology, but not a gospel."[6]

Connecting the kingdom of God to Christ's person and work is important because many people think of Christianity merely as a set of timeless principles. But that's not the message of Scripture. Like a stick of dynamite dropped into the ground, the gospel explodes any understanding built on our morality and works. Christianity is not ultimately about a system of beliefs or principles of morality but about a person—Jesus—and how he accomplished something in history that will shape all of eternity. Jesus doesn't give us instructions to build a kingdom; he announces that he is the king, and that in knowing and belonging to him, God's reign comes through God's people over all God's creation.

The good news is not only *that* the kingdom has come, but also *who* it is coming through. But *how* does Christ bring the kingdom? Answering that question will be the focus of the rest of this chapter.

THE SERVANT KING

Jesus is the kingdom personified.[7] But when contemporary ears hear "kingdom," many think of a physical place with geographic boundaries or perhaps a heavenly palace with clouds and pearly gates. Whatever image comes to mind when you hear the word "kingdom," replace it with a mental picture of a person, Jesus. Imagine Jesus healing a body deteriorated by disease. Think of Jesus removing the burden of guilt and shame. Picture Jesus setting free the oppressed. When you hear "kingdom," don't imagine a palace in the sky, think of a person on the ground bringing restoration to a world marred by sin. As the Nigerian theologian Victor Babajide Cole says, "Jesus' very presence brought the kingdom near."[8]

God Doesn't Meet Us Halfway

Is Jesus God or is he man? Yes. He is the eternal God who became man. The theological word for this is *incarnation*. It's a huge concept, but it will help to break down the word. *Carne* means meat or flesh (think *carne asada* or *chili con carne*). The in-carnation is about God "in meat" or God "in the flesh." The eternal Son of God took on human flesh, becoming fully human while remaining fully God. It's glorious and mind-bending. And that means, contrary to popular belief, that God doesn't meet us halfway. He has come all the way. Though we fail miserably in our striving to ascend God's throne, the kingdom descends to us in grace.

The kingdom of God comes through the Son of God. Jesus left his throne in heaven, but he did not cease to be king. He came as king, behind enemy lines, to serve notice that God was retaking what had always been his. Christ's royalty was hidden under the garb of a Galilean rabbi, but it was always there. Jesus reigns, but not like other monarchs. He reigns by serving rather than demanding to be served. He is powerful, but his power is guided by his love. He is just, but his justice is coupled with mercy. He is wise, but his ways are so counterintuitive to our selfish hearts that the world perceives his wisdom as folly.

Miracles, Not Magic Tricks

Jesus is not a magician who came to entertain; he is the Messiah who saves. The miracles, healings, and exorcisms of Jesus are all glimpses of that comprehensive salvation. Jesus fed people to meet their temporal needs, but he also said, "I am the bread of life" who can satisfy eternal needs (John 6:35). He gave water to quench temporary thirst, but he also claimed that he was "the living water" who can quench spiritual thirst (John 7:37). Jesus healed people to bring physical relief from pain and suffering, but he also said, "I am the resurrection" (John 11:25) who gives eternal life. The miracles of Jesus are not magic tricks; they are in-breakings of the kingdom of God.

In Jesus's day, most people expected the kingdom to come all at once, like flipping a switch from dark to light. But with Jesus, wherever he went, the kingdom was gradually breaking in. Jesus cast out demons, displaying the power of his reign over the spiritual realm. He healed the deaf, blind, and lame, showing that God's kingdom restores the fullness of God's creation purposes. He multiplied loaves of bread and fish to feed thousands of people, demonstrating that the king not only provides, but he lavishes with abundance.

Jesus didn't come to make the world a better place. He came to make the world new by grace. Like rays of sun that pierce through the dark clouds, the healings and miracles of Jesus are God's reign breaking in on earth as it is in heaven. Each miraculous act is a microcosm of what God's power will one day do for the whole universe.

Jesus, the Storyteller

Jesus was a remarkable teacher. He explained concepts. He answered questions. But most of all, he told stories. When Jesus wanted to teach his disciples about anything, and especially when he wanted to teach them about the kingdom, he would tell a story. Jesus told many stories, and he would often begin them by saying, "The kingdom of God is like . . ."

Jesus once said the kingdom of God is like a mustard seed. The mustard seed is the smallest of seeds, yet when planted in the ground it grows bigger than many other trees (Matt. 13:31–32). With stories like this, Jesus was teaching his followers that the kingdom may start small, with a poor Galilean carpenter and his group of unimpressive disciples, but it would grow and bear fruit greater than any other institution or movement in history, reaching all people groups of the world.

Jesus told another story about how the kingdom of God is like leaven (or yeast) hidden in dough (Matt. 13:33). Expanding on the image of the tiny mustard seed, he taught that even when the kingdom grows, it does so in a way that is hidden from the wisdom of the world. Like yeast expanding in bread, when followers of Jesus exhibit humility and service, the kingdom advances, even though it may be perceived as weakness to the world. The kingdom starts small, grows gradually in the face of adversity, and will one day reach a glorious culmination in a new creation.

Jesus told many more stories about the kingdom of God, teaching his disciples that his kingdom is like no other kingdom. Every parable was a window giving a glimpse into the kingdom and a doorway inviting all to enter in and follow the king.

A Perfect Life, for Us

Jesus lived a perfect life. That doesn't mean he never had a bad hair day or didn't have to learn how to walk, talk, or read. He was, after all, fully human. To say that he was perfect means that he always kept God's covenant, he never broke God's law, and he lived for the glory of God with every thought, attitude, and action. Jesus was "without sin" (Heb. 4:15), and in all that he did he loved God and neighbor.

Through his perfect life, Jesus was redoing what Adam and Israel had failed to do.

Adam chose his own way in the garden of Eden.
Jesus chose God's way in the garden of Gethsemane.

Israel failed the test in the wilderness.
Jesus was faithful when tempted in the wilderness.

Adam and Israel abandoned the mission of the kingdom of God.
Jesus embodied the kingdom of God.

Jesus is the "second Adam" and the "true Israel" who fulfills every promise of God. And yet his perfect life is *for us*. He kept the covenant on our behalf so that he could not only forgive us of our sins but also give us his righteousness. By grace, his perfect life is reckoned to us. "For our sake he made him to be sin who knew no sin, so that in him we might become the righteousness of God" (2 Cor. 5:21).

THE CRUCIFIED KING

For three years Jesus proclaimed the kingdom, displayed its power, and extended its reach. His movement grew. Momentum was building. The long-awaited kingdom of God was about to arrive in fullness!

Then Jesus was killed.

His followers were demoralized, and their pain was matched only by their confusion. How could he have died? Why was he defeated? What now? Pulling the lifeless body of their king off the tree on which he hung, his followers assumed that the kingdom movement was over. What could sacrificial death have to do with royal victory?

The Kingdom through the Cross

The kingdom mission of Jesus certainly appeared to come to a halt at the cross. So how do we understand the seemingly conflicting messages of the kingdom and the cross?

One of Jesus's disciples, a man named Mark, helped God's people understand the answer to this question. He wrote a short account, summarizing the life and ministry of Jesus. The first half of Mark's Gospel is about Jesus proclaiming and demonstrating the kingdom. The second half is about the cross. Yet throughout his narrative, Mark subtly yet powerfully shows that the cross is not a stumbling stone to the kingdom of God; it is its cornerstone.

The cross is the climax of a story that begins in the garden and culminates in the kingdom.

Garden ————————  ———————— Kingdom

The crucifixion scene is filled with royal imagery. Jesus is given a purple robe, a scepter in his hand, and a crown of thorns on his head (Mark 15:17; see also Matt. 27:28–29). Even as he hangs on the cross, the sign above his head reads, "The King of the Jews" (Mark 15:26). Mark is showing through irony that the one mocked as king truly is king. But he's a different kind of king. The onlookers ridicule Jesus, saying, "Save yourself, and come down from the cross!" (v. 30). Yet Jesus revealed his kingship not by coming down from the cross to save himself but by staying on the cross to save others. The cross is the greatest display of Christ's reign as power controlled by love.

The disciples didn't understand what was truly happening, but the most unlikely person—one of the Roman guards who was killing Jesus—caught the significance. He looked up at this suffering messiah and attributed to him a royal title: "Truly this man was the Son of God!" (v. 39). While the world rejected Jesus, this Roman soldier looked at the crucified Christ and saw the kingdom of God. The cross is the throne from which the king of the world rules with grace.

Mark was showing us that the cross did not derail Jesus and his kingdom work. Jesus is king *on* the cross: forgiving sin, defeating evil, and establishing God's kingdom on earth as it is in heaven. The cross is neither the failure of Jesus's messianic ministry, nor is it a prelude to his royal glory. It is the apex of his kingdom mission. The splendor of God's royal power shines brightest through the sacrificial death of the Son of God. The cross is the crowning achievement of Christ's kingdom mission.

A Multifaceted Accomplishment

Understanding the cross in light of the kingdom helps us to see more of the fullness of its glory. As the Sri Lankan theologian Prabo Mihindukulasuriya says, "Jesus inaugurated the kingdom on the cross, which would enable us to understand better the gospel's integral content and the atonement's kaleidoscopic images."[9] Like a diamond refracting different colors as light shines through it, the cross needs to be appreciated as a multifaceted, many-splendored accomplishment.

Through the cross . . .
God demonstrates his love.
God reveals his justice.
God satisfied his wrath.
God displays his wisdom.
God magnifies his glory.

We are redeemed from slavery.
We are forgiven of guilt.
We are cleansed of shame.
We are declared righteous.
We are ransomed from death.
We are adopted into a family.

Death is defeated.
Satan is conquered.
Demons are vanquished.
Evil is eradicated.
The world is reconciled.
Creation is renewed.
Heaven and earth come together.

The death of Christ is a multifaceted accomplishment within the narrative of God bringing his kingdom on earth as it is in heaven.

While the accomplishments of the cross are unending, the heart of the cross, out of which everything else flows, is substitutionary atonement. Substitutionary atonement might sound academic, but it is not difficult to understand. It means that Christ died for our sins in our place (substitution) to make us "at-one" or reconciled with God (atonement).[10] Let's break this down even further.

In the entirety of his life, Jesus was perfectly obedient, faithful, and righteous. Through the cross, Jesus offered his perfect, covenant-keeping life as an unblemished sacrifice on our behalf. He is the only one who did not have sins of his own that deserved judgment. Nevertheless, Jesus voluntarily went to the cross in our place to bear the judgment for our sins.

> He was pierced for our transgressions;
>   he was crushed for our iniquities;
> upon him was the chastisement that brought us peace,
>   and with his wounds we are healed. (Isa. 53:5)

This passage, like many others that refer to Christ's death, draws from sacrificial atonement imagery found throughout the history of Israel. In the Old Testament, an unblemished lamb would bear the sins of the people by dying in their place. The lamb would receive the judgment for sins, and the people would be forgiven of their sins. Jesus is the "lamb of God, who takes away the sin of the world" (John 1:29). Christ's death reveals that grace is free, but it's not cheap; it cost Jesus his life. This is not sentimental love; it is sacrificial love.

In the New Testament, we see even more clearly that substitutionary atonement is not only a pardon but an exchange. Christ takes our sin; we receive his righteousness. He takes our shame; we receive his honor. He takes our guilt; we receive his perfect record. The innocent was condemned as guilty so the guilty could be declared innocent. When Jesus wipes away our sins, he doesn't just give us a clean slate; he gives us a new heart, a new nature, and a new power—the Holy Spirit. It's for good reason that the early church called this "the sweet exchange"![11]

The death of Christ is the climax of the world's story and the hinge on which our lives turn.

The cross transforms us because it transfers us . . .
from death to life,
from bondage to freedom,
from shame to honor,
from mourning to dancing,
from darkness to light,
from fear to faith,
from ashes to beauty,
from defeat to victory.

A Cross-Shaped Kingdom

Dietrich Bonhoeffer once said, "A king who dies on the cross must be the king of a rather strange kingdom."[12] A strange kingdom indeed; for while the kingdoms of this world are built by force, the kingdom of God is founded on grace. Since God's kingdom is founded on and forever shaped by the cross of Christ, we can say it truly is a cross-shaped kingdom.

The cross-shaped kingdom of Christ provides a framework for those who follow Christ as king. Jesus says, "If anyone would come after me, let him deny himself and take up his cross daily and follow me" (Luke 9:23). To follow the king, we have to take up our crosses. The kingdom was established through the self-giving love of Christ, and it will be advanced through the self-giving love of his people. The kingdom comes through suffering and service.

Followers of Jesus are bound for glory. But what is true for Christ is also true for those who are "in Christ": glory comes through suffering. As coheirs of the kingdom with Christ, "we suffer with him in order that we may also be glorified with him" (Rom. 8:17). As Martin Luther King Jr. said, "Christianity has always insisted that the cross we bear always precedes the crown we wear."[13]

THE RESURRECTED KING

Jesus died for our sins. But Christianity rises or falls on whether or not Jesus still has a heartbeat. The apostle Paul wrote, "If Christ has not been raised, your faith is futile and you are still in your sins" (1 Cor. 15:17). If Jesus is still dead, then our faith is fake, our guilt is real, and our hope is naive optimism. If the tomb is not empty, our story is nothing but a religious fairy tale, helpful only for numbing the pain in a life that's too hard to bear.

But Jesus is not dead. The tomb is empty. Christ died on the cross for our sins, but he didn't stay there. He rose from the grave, defeating sin, Satan, and death. Just as the sun rises over creation, the Son of God rose as the dawn of the new creation. Jesus walked out of the tomb, and he has been changing lives ever since. The kingdom is advancing because the king is alive.

What is the deeper meaning of the resurrection in the kingdom story?

Vindication

Jesus' royal identity and mission are proven

Participation

In Christ, we experience the power of resurrection

New Creation

Jesus is the beginning of the renewed cosmos

Vindication

People often think of the resurrection as a last-minute triumph that unexpectedly saved the day after Christ was crushed on the cross. But this misunderstands Christ's work. The cross is not a defeat that is made right by the resurrection but a victory that is revealed in the resurrection. Christ's resurrection is the *vindication* of his mission.

To be vindicated means that you are proven right when you appear to be in the wrong. I was recently with a group of friends, and I made the claim that Kevin Durant, NBA Finals MVP for the Golden State Warriors, was originally drafted by the Seattle Supersonics. No one believed me. Some even laughed. But then I pulled out my phone and found a picture of Kevin Durant wearing number 35 in his Supersonics uniform. I was vindicated! Everyone thought I was wrong, but Google proved that I was right.

When Jesus died on the cross, everyone thought he was wrong about who he claimed to be and what he came to do. Jesus said he was the Messiah, the promised Savior who would bring God's kingdom through God's people over God's creation. This claim was in question after Jesus was crucified and placed in a tomb. But when Jesus rose from the grave, he was vindicated— proven right all along. Romans 1:4 says that Jesus "was declared to be the Son of God in power according to the Spirit of holiness by his resurrection from the dead." It doesn't say he *became* the Son of God through his resurrection. He was *declared* the Son of God, vindicated as the savior king.

Participation

The resurrection means that Christianity isn't based merely on a historical figure but on a living Savior. And because he's alive, we can experience the rich and abundant life he came to bring us. In Galatians 2:20 Paul wrote, "I have been crucified with Christ. It is no longer I who live, but Christ who lives in me." Those who follow Christ belong to him and are united with the risen and reigning king in his death and resurrection. The same power that raised Christ from the dead is available to us through faith.

Many Christians believe in the resurrection but live like Jesus is still in the tomb. They may believe intellectually that he rose, but for all practical purposes he is uninvolved, as if he went back into the tomb for a nap. If Jesus is alive, it means there is power available to us that is greater than any challenge or obstacles we will ever face. This power is not a force to be wielded, though;

he's a person to be known. The power for the Christian life is found in knowing Christ.

My kids first learned about the reality of death by using my iPhone. When the phone stops working, my four-year old daughter will say, "It's dead." But she also knows the solution to iPhone death. She knows that for the phone to "have life" again, it must be connected to a source of power.

My iPhone can teach us a lesson about life. Jesus is the eternal source of power and life. The way to experience the resurrection life of Jesus is by staying connected to him. The life we long for was achieved through his resurrection and is only experienced by being united to him.

New Creation

The resurrection is about vindication and participation, but also new creation. God's people had always longed for the promised renewal of the heavens and the earth, and they expected it all to happen at once at the end of time. But when Jesus rose from the grave, the new creation broke through into the middle of the story. The bodily resurrection of Christ is the beginning of a worldwide resurrection. As the Brazilian theologian Leonardo Boff says, "The resurrection is a process that began with Jesus and that will go on until it embraces all creation."[14] The resurrection of Christ is the beginning of the renovation of the cosmos.

Jesus rose from the grave and ascended into heaven, where he sat down at the right hand of his Father. He sat down to show that he had accomplished what he came to do. But he didn't sit in a La-Z-Boy; he sat on a throne. He still reigns! Through his Word and Spirit, he rules the world today by applying and continuing the work he accomplished with this life, death, and resurrection. Jesus is the beginning of the new creation, and one day by his gracious reign, he will bring resurrection renewal to the whole earth.

I've tried to explain the meaning of Christ's saving work. But sometimes only poetry can enable us to fully grasp the beauty and power of the gospel.

Against the light of the world,
the gloomy little tomb never stood a chance.
So when the stone was rolled away,
the darkness ran away.

That's when hope walked out of the tomb.
That's when love showed itself incorruptible.
That's when faith became sight.

The man from Nazareth is who he said he was—
the king of creation.
He accomplished what he said he would—
he made a kingdom of all nations.

He defeated death through death.
He conquered evil through love.
He beat the enemy through sacrifice.
And brought the kingdom from above.

The cross was the apex but not the final destination.
The resurrection of Christ begins the world's renovation.
The grave is empty, and the world is full of meaning.
There's a void in the tomb, so we've got a reason to
    keep singing.

If death didn't stop Jesus,
then I don't know what can.
No matter what comes our way,
he will accomplish his plan.

Apart from God's grace,
this would never be a given.
But thank God that it's true,
he is risen.

A KINGDOM TAKES THE SHAPE OF ITS KING

As we've seen, a kingdom without a king is really no kingdom at all. Apart from Christ the king, Christianity becomes a self-help spirituality, a hobby, a family tradition, or an escape mechanism from the difficulties of life. Apart from Jesus, doctrine is mere theory, good works become religious badges, and the church turns into a social club.

But with Christ the king, the kingdom is unstoppable. The kingdom of Jesus can take on the worst evil and suffering the world can throw at it, and bring life from death, beauty from ashes, and wisdom from folly. With Christ as the source and center, the kingdom has abundant life, sacrificial love, and resurrection power. And while the kingdom was glimpsed throughout Christ's life, it was established for all eternity through his death, and it's available to us today because of his resurrection.

Chapter 4

THE MAJESTIC IN THE
MUNDANE

Nothing matters but the kingdom, but because of the kingdom everything matters.

Gordon Spykman, *Reformational Theology*

Stephen Hawking devoted his life to a project that pushed the boundaries of science, seeking nothing less than a "theory of everything."[1] According to Hawking, who was an atheist, it is insufficient for scientists to explain *how* the universe works; they must also know *why* it exists. As a physicist, Hawking shined as he explained how the universe is held together with gravity, electromagnetic forces, and strong and weak nuclear forces. But when he got to his explanation for "why" the universe exists, his theory lost coherence and he struggled to give purpose or direction. According to Hawking, we are purely material creatures whose experiences of love, joy, and meaning are nothing but neurons firing in our brains. As he exclaimed in an interview, "The human race is just a chemical scum on a moderate-sized planet."[2]

Stephen Hawking's theory of everything may not explain the *why* of life, but there is another place to turn for answers. Jesus offers his own theory of everything—a comprehensive vision for how and why we live. It's called the kingdom of God.

The kingdom is a vision for God's reign over *all* of life. God's reign begins in the human heart, but it doesn't end there. One day it will spread to the ends of the earth, and until that day, Jesus calls us to bring every aspect of our lives into submission to his gracious reign. As the Ecuadorian theologian René Padilla says, "The gospel is the good news concerning the kingdom, and the kingdom is God's rule over the totality of life."[3]

But there's a problem.

Most Christians are experts at compartmentalizing their lives.

OUR COMPARTMENTALIZED FAITH

We all compartmentalize. Just think of your closet or your dresser. The shirts go here, the pants there. Your socks have a drawer, and your shoes have their own spot. Everything is in its place, organized into compartments.

To some extent we all do this with our lives as well. Imagine your life as a dresser. There's a drawer for work, and another one for friends. Dreams go in one slot while fears belong in another. And then, to complete our well-rounded wardrobe, we have a drawer for Jesus. He gets the "spiritual" or "religious" compartment, the one we pull out on Sunday mornings, or when we're in a crisis and need an answer to prayer.

This type of compartmentalized thinking leads to a view of the world where we see some things as sacred and other things as secular. We believe God cares about spiritual things like church, prayer, and Chick-fil-A, but activities like our career, our hobbies, or our love for sports are neutral. We think they only matter to God if they are used for higher spiritual purposes like sharing our faith with a coworker or saying a prayer before a game.

The danger with this approach is that it fails to honor the

claim of Jesus that all of life belongs to him. We may claim Jesus as king but then draw clear lines around his jurisdiction. "I give my life—at least the spiritual parts—to Jesus." "Jesus is king, but only of my Sunday mornings and when I pray or read my Bible." We claim Christ as king, but we treat him like an accessory. Here's the truth: when we don't give *everything* over to Jesus, we're still the one who is in control. We act as our own king and then try to use Jesus to accomplish our goals.

Have you heard what Thomas Jefferson did to the Bible and the teachings of Jesus? He took his Bible in one hand and a pair of scissors in the other and cut out all the parts he disagreed with. For Jefferson this mostly involved cutting out anything supernatural like the miracles of Jesus. We might think to ourselves, "Oh, I would never do something like that." But we do! We do this by the way we live our lives, ignoring or disregarding whole parts of Scripture. Augustine once said, "If you believe what you like in the Gospels, and reject what you don't like, it is not the gospel you believe, but yourself."[4] We need to step down from the throne and recognize that where Jesus reigns, he reigns over all.

CHRIST'S COMPREHENSIVE REIGN

Jesus did not leave his heavenly throne and go to the cross to become Lord of your "spiritual life." Jesus gave all of himself, and he demands all of you. Saying that Jesus is lord of your spiritual life is like saying you're on a diet when you're not eating. It means nothing. Following Christ as king means to surrender every aspect of your life to him—work, relationships, politics, family, your past, your future—everything. Colossians 1:15–20 proclaims Christ as the creator, sustainer, and reconciler of "all things." Everything that exists was made through him and for him.

Trees, people, enchiladas, the solar system, marriage, guitars—everything exists for Jesus and his glory.

Jesus will not settle for being your spiritual butler.

He is king of creation.

Jesus does not fit into your "religious" compartment.

He is king of creation.

Jesus is not merely the leader of a religion.

He is king of creation.

It's time to do away with the ridiculous idea of a privatized faith. Christianity is deeply personal, but it is not private. Christianity is a public and prophetic faith, speaking not only to individual souls but to our communities, to our culture, and to the world. What if Martin Luther King Jr., the great civil rights leader who fought for racial equality, had kept his faith private? What if William Wilberforce, the British parliamentarian who gave his life to end the slave trade and the practice of slavery through the British Empire, had kept his faith private? What if Mother Teresa, who worked tirelessly to care for the poor on the streets of Calcutta, had kept her faith private?

To surrender to the kingdom of Christ is to live under his comprehensive reign. Irenaeus of Lyons wrote, "The Son of God was . . . procuring for us a comprehensive salvation, that we might recover in Christ Jesus what in Adam we had lost."[5] This all-encompassing reign of Christ means that we must bring the gospel to bear on every aspect of our beings (minds, bodies, souls) and in every facet of life (spiritual, relational, social, etc.).

Sometimes I get nervous when I hear people say, "Jesus reigns in my heart." I'm apprehensive because our culture uses the word *heart* very differently than the Bible does. In our vernacular, *heart* usually refers to feelings or emotions. Following your heart means surrendering to your desires or following your gut instinct. So, if saying "Jesus reigns in my heart" means "Jesus reigns over my feelings," then we have a problem. Jesus is king over our emotions, but his rule should not stop there.

In Scripture, the heart is the seat of the emotions, the intellect, and the will. It is the control room of the inner person, shaping every aspect of life. What happens in the heart is determinative of the rest, so if Jesus gets your heart, he gets all of you. Jesus doesn't just reign *in* the heart, he reigns *from* the heart. He claims authority over all.

The Dutch theologian Abraham Kuyper put it well when he said, "There is not a square inch in the whole domain of our human existence over which Christ, who is sovereign over all, does not cry, 'Mine!'"[6] Our compartmentalized faith must give way to Christ's comprehensive reign. Imagine what your life could look like if the power of the kingdom were infused into your day-to-day routines. It's possible. Let's learn how.

WORK

If a person went to church every Sunday from the age of twenty-five to age sixty-five, he or she would spend around three-thousand hours gathered with the body of Christ. If the same person worked full-time during that span, he or she would put in around eighty-thousand work hours. My point? It is the work-place, not the sanctuary, where most Christians live out their faith. If God's reign shapes *all of life*, then it must shape one's view of work.

How does faith in Christ inform our work? Many people immediately think of sharing the gospel in the office or making loads of money to give to ministry and missions. While neither of those are wrong, a kingdom vision of God's reign over all of life instills our work with greater meaning and motivation.

God Is at Work in Our Work

Many people think of God's work in the world solely in terms of spiritual salvation. And while spiritual salvation is essential, the biblical vision of the kingdom of God is not about plucking souls from a fallen creation; it is about God saving people in his renewal of creation. God is constantly at work in sustaining and renewing the world, and he does much of his work through us, often working through our work.

The Bible says the Lord "gives food to every creature" (Ps. 136:25 NIV). But how does he feed them? God doesn't snap his fingers and make food appear on a plate. Rather, he feeds people through the farmer, the truck driver, the grocer, the cook, and the server. As Martin Luther said, "God could easily give you grain and fruit without your plowing and planting, but he does not want to do so."[7] God provides through the vocations of people. He is milking the cow through the vocation of the milkmaid, as Luther argued.

God Cares about All Work

This means that all types of work matter in the kingdom of God. Jesus is working through the vocations of his people, who are salt and light in the industries where the Lord has placed them, witnessing in the way they do their work to a better kingdom. That's why in Scripture many of God's people have vocations that would be considered "secular" today. Joseph was in politics, Daniel was a student, Boaz was a businessman, Nehemiah was a city planner, Lydia was a designer, and Jesus was a carpenter.

According to Amy Sherman, God is at work in the world in a variety of ways, and the myriad of human vocations give expression to the different aspects of God's work. Sherman offers several categories to help think through different types of vocational callings:[8]

God's Work
in Our Vocations

- **Redemptive work:** God's saving and reconciling actions
  - pastors
  - counselors
  - peacemakers
- **Creative work:** God's fashioning of the physical and human world
  - musicians
  - poets
  - painters
  - architects
  - interior designers
- **Providential work:** God's provision for and sustaining of humans and creation
  - mechanics
  - plumbers
  - firefighters
- **Justice work:** God's maintenance of justice
  - judges
  - lawyers
  - law enforcement
- **Compassionate work:** God's involvement in comforting, healing, guiding, and shepherding
  - doctors
  - nurses
  - paramedics
  - psychologists
  - social workers
- **Revelatory work:** God's work to enlighten with truth
  - educators
  - scientists
  - journalists

How do we discover our individual callings within this holistic vision of work? A good place to start is by pondering the words of Frederick Buechner: "The place God calls you to is the place where your deep gladness and the world's deep hunger meet."[9] Whatever you do, whether as a pastor or a painter, do it for the glory of God (1 Cor. 10:31; Col. 3:23).

Excellence in Character and Craft

One way to avoid the sacred/secular divide that we talked about earlier is to remember that "Christian" works better as a noun than as an adjective. For example, there is no such thing as "Christian coffee," even if it's served in a café called Grounded in Christ or Bean Redeemed. There are Christians, and some of them make good coffee and some make terrible coffee. The same is true for filmmakers, musicians, nurses, dentists, and almost any vocation you can consider. If you have put your faith in Christ, you *are* a Christian and you are called to be a good steward of whatever the Lord has entrusted to you vocationally, whether a scalpel or an electric guitar. Pursue excellence in your character and your craft.

When our work is understood within the story of the kingdom, people will want to be lawyers because they care about justice and not social status, doctors because they care about health and not wealth, businesspersons because they care about people and not profit, and artists because they value beauty and not celebrity.

For many people today, work is a way of building our own kingdom and making a name for ourselves. The gospel frees us from looking to our work as a way of justifying ourselves and allows us to see work for what it was meant to be: a calling from God to use our gifts and abilities to serve others and our society.

REST

We are busy people living in a frenzied culture. We are addicted to hurry, starved for time, overscheduled, and exhausted. Just ask someone, "How are you doing?" and one of the most common replies you'll get is a sigh followed by "busy." And yet, as we run on the treadmill of busyness, we try to avoid thinking about the fact that we're usually not going anywhere. But while it is easy to point out *that* we are busy, it is more important to ask *why* we are so busy.

The Treadmill of Busyness

We make ourselves busy because it makes us feel important. How else would we prove our value and worth in a performance-driven culture where we are defined by how much we produce? So we never stop working.

In our culture we've turned busyness into a virtue. But others have long recognized the dangers of the overcommitted life. Socrates said, "Beware the barrenness of a busy life." Augustine saw that the deeper problem behind the frantic life is a frenzied heart: "Our hearts are restless until they find rest in [God]."[10] The answer to busyness is not simply a weekend getaway or the latest time-management system. We need a deeper solution, something that gets to the level of our soul but still plays out practically in day-to-day life.

Resting in God's Royalty

Our ability to rest is directly related to our faith in God's ability to reign. If we really believe that God is the sovereign king over all, then we can take a break from our work because we trust that while we rest, he still reigns. If you stop working, the world keeps going.

The biblical word behind this concept of rest is *sabbath*, and it comes from a Hebrew verb that means to cease or to stop. Sabbath rest is about hitting the pause button on life so you can focus on dwelling and delighting in God. Seven hours of Facebook stalking is not what God intends by sabbath. Netflix binging is unlikely to give your soul the refreshment it needs. But true rest is more than just doing nothing; it is deliberately slowing down to refocus on what matters most. We pause from our work to dwell in the king's presence and delight in his goodness.

Resting reinforces that our identity is *received* rather than *achieved*. By accepting God's invitation to rest and delight in his presence, we learn who we are apart from our efforts to justify ourselves. Sabbath rest is a megaphone to our performance-driven culture that our value is not determined by how much we accomplish. We have been called out of a world trying to prove its worth and value by what it does or possesses. We are deeply loved by God not for what we do but for who we are. The Sabbath rest that we have enables us to be human *beings* rather than human *doings*.

Are you tired? Stressed? Overwhelmed? Jesus says, "Come to me, all who labor and are heavy laden, and I will give you rest" (Matt. 11:28). Our rest, therefore, is not ultimately in a day of the week, but in a person—Jesus—who is the same yesterday, today, and forever. In Christ we have rest that is not dependent on the circumstances of life.

This inner rest then manifests itself outwardly in rhythms of rest and in habits that cultivate peace in our lives. In other words, this understanding of rest affects your soul and your schedule. I recommend taking at least one day per week and one week per year and setting it aside for rest and refreshment. An essential aspect of resting in our digital age is regularly unplugging from technology. A regular social-media sabbath trains us to be present in the moment and disallows a helpful instrument from becoming a replacement for embodied relationships. It's not that these electronic devices are bad, but we need regular rhythms that keep our hearts from turning tools into distraction devices. These rhythms of rest will bring peace and perspective in our lives.

PLAY

When I was eighteen years old, I had two great loves: Jesus and basketball. To be honest, I had no idea how or if they were related to each other. Usually it felt like they were in competition. My compartmentalized world clearly placed basketball in the "secular" category—a neutral activity at best, the devil's workshop at worst. But I knew there was more to the game than winning and losing. I wondered, *Does God care about sports?*

I set out on a journey to answer that question, and the more I learned about the kingdom of God, the more I understood why God does, in fact, care about sports.

More Than a Game

We are created to play. The opening chapters of the Bible reveal that humans are wired with creativity and invited to revel in the goodness of God's creation. It's no surprise, therefore, that every child has a natural impulse to play and every culture develops games and contests. Play—and what would eventually develop into sports—are part of God's good design and intention for his creation.[11]

Most people think that sports are neutral in and of themselves but have the potential to be good *if* they are used for higher, spiritual purposes such as moral training or evangelism. This is the world where the be-all and end-all of faith and sports is thanking God after the game (usually only after a win). According to this view, sports have only *instrumental* value; they are good if they are used as an instrument for evangelism. But as we learned,

God's image bearers are not only called to develop God's creation for the good of others; we are also called to delight in God's creation itself. Sports can be used for many good things, but they are made good in and of themselves. Sports do not only have *instrumental* worth; they have *intrinsic* worth. We are created to play, and like a father who builds a sandbox for his children, God is honored and takes joy when his sons and daughters delight in his workmanship.

Less Than a God

Sports are a good gift from God. But when a good thing becomes an ultimate thing, thereby replacing God himself, it then becomes a destructive thing. Sports are a good hobby, maybe even a great job, but they are a bad god. If you look to sports for your identity, value, and meaning in life, you will be disappointed. For many people today, success in sports—or even the success of their favorite team—is an idol to which they are willing to sacrifice their time and energy to satisfy.

A Gift to Be Enjoyed

The gospel transforms the way we think of sports.[12] By God's grace, we receive a new identity and a new purpose in life. Sports no longer have to be ultimate for us. I'll be disappointed if I lose the game, but I won't be crushed because I know my identity isn't based on winning or success. When the pressure is off sports to bring meaning and value to our lives, then we can receive sports for what they were meant to be, a gift.

If you want to glorify God in sports, you don't have to name your team the God Squad or only cheer for Christian athletes. You don't have to limit your involvement to *church* basketball leagues. Why? Because God made us to be fully human and to creatively enjoy the goodness of his creation. This world is the playground of God's goodness and the arena of his glory.

The joy of sports is not only for life today. I believe we will play sports in the new creation forever. God is renewing his original intention for the way the world was meant to be, and that means we will be finding new and even better ways to play in eternity. I can't wait to play basketball in the new creation. In the meantime, play foreshadows the joy of the kingdom when Christ will reign over all, and decay, disease, and death will be no more.[13]

FOOD

Sitting down for a meal might seem like a mundane, nonspiritual type of activity. Especially within a sacred/secular mind-set that values the spiritual over the material, food is often considered mere fuel for the body. In Scripture, however, food plays a significant role in the kingdom of God. That's why at the end of the story, the kingdom of God is portrayed as a great wedding banquet with the choicest of foods (Rev. 19:6–9). Why is food so important in the kingdom of God, and how can that shape our daily lives?

Taste Buds Were God's Idea

God could have made food bland and tasteless. He could have given us a pill to take daily. He could have made people who simply needed to plug in to recharge and replenish. But he didn't. He made food with a variety of tastes, and he made people with taste buds. Scientists call these "taste receptors," and your tongue has anywhere between two thousand and eight thousand of them. Every time you bite into a strawberry or an avocado, those taste receptors are stimulated, sending a message to your brain that makes you feel pleasure. You are wired to receive joy, constantly and consistently.

God has given food as a gift for us to enjoy. The gift is meant ultimately to reveal and invite us into the richness of the Giver.

"Oh, taste and see that the LORD is good!" (Ps. 34:8). Food is a sign pointing to a greater reality: God himself. Every bite is an opportunity to delight in God and his goodness. Every glorious combination of different foods—peanut butter and jelly, chips and salsa, spaghetti and meatballs—is another reason to take joy in the Giver of every good gift.

Food is more than fuel. That's why God—the greatest culinary genius of all time—says, "Eat what is good, and delight yourselves in rich food" (Isa. 55:2).

A Deadly Sin

In a world marred by sin, that which is meant to bring life can be twisted into an instrument of sickness and even death. There are eating disorders and addiction, but perhaps the most common way that food becomes unhealthy is gluttony. While most people simply associate gluttony with overeating, it is really a much deeper problem. Gluttony is *when we look for physical means to solve spiritual or emotional problems.* When someone is grieving and they run to food (rather than God) for comfort, that food has become an idol. When someone escapes dealing with pain by numbing it with alcohol, they are missing the opportunity to take their pain to God and experience healing. Frederick Buechner says, "A glutton is one who raids the icebox for a cure for spiritual malnutrition."[14] Food is a gift from God. But don't look to food for something it cannot give you.

Jesus and the Meaning of a Meal

Sharing meals was a significant aspect of Jesus's ministry. Notice, for example, how Luke reports Jesus doing most of his ministry in the context of table fellowship.

- Luke 5—Jesus eats with tax collectors and sinners at the home of Levi.

- Luke 7—Jesus is anointed at the home of Simon the Pharisee during a meal.
- Luke 9—Jesus feeds the five thousand.
- Luke 10—Jesus eats in the home of Martha and Mary.
- Luke 11—Jesus condemns the Pharisees at a meal.
- Luke 14—Jesus is at a meal when he urges people to invite the poor, rather than friends, to their meals.
- Luke 19—Jesus invites himself to dinner with Zacchaeus.
- Luke 22—Jesus institutes the Lord's Supper.
- Luke 24—The risen Christ eats with two disciples in Emmaus and then later eats with the disciples in Jerusalem.

Robert Karris concludes, "In Luke's gospel Jesus is either going to a meal, at a meal, or coming from a meal."[15] You might even say Jesus was a foodie (*Merriam-Webster* defines a *foodie* as "a person who enjoys and cares about food very much").

Why is food so significant? It's not the intake of carbohydrates and protein alone that makes food meaningful. Sharing a meal represents sharing life. The English word *companion* comes from the Latin *com* ("with") and *panis* ("bread") meaning a person with whom you eat bread. Sharing a meal is very personal, and that's why the most important events in life (birthdays, weddings, and parties) always include food. If you want to get to know someone, you don't say, "Would you like to get together and communicate with one another?" Instead, you say, "Let's get coffee or a bite to eat." Every meal is an opportunity for growing and developing our relationships, sharing our lives, serving others, enjoying God's blessings, and communing with God and others. Sounds like a picture of God's kingdom, doesn't it?

Feasting Forever in the Kingdom

The end goal of God's kingdom, as we learn in the Bible, is not a disembodied existence but a new creation. This means there will be food and cooking and feasting throughout eternity. When Revelation says that the kings will bring their cultures into the new creation (Rev. 21:24), I have great joy and anticipation that there will be Mexican food there.

The hope for the new creation includes detailed descriptions of the food and feasting that will take place:

> On this mountain the LORD Almighty will prepare
>   a feast of rich food for all peoples,
> a banquet of aged wine—
>   the best of meats and the finest of wines.
>
> He will swallow up death forever.
> The Sovereign LORD will wipe away the tears
>   from all faces;
> he will remove his people's disgrace
>   from all the earth. (Isa. 25:6, 8 NIV)

Living under the reign of the resurrected king, we begin to view food from a kingdom perspective. Every bite we take is a foretaste of the eternal joy available in Christ. Every meal is a reminder that we have a place at God's table. The king has invited us to his banquet, where we will feast on the most delicious food with the best of friends in the presence of the greatest source of joy himself. We will be satisfied, and God will be glorified.

ART

Makoto Fujimura, a Japanese artist who revels in the beauty of the kingdom of God, tells a story that illustrates how art is more than an extracurricular activity for the people of God. During graduate school, Fujimura and his wife were scraping by financially, living paycheck to paycheck when one day he came home and noticed flowers on the dining room table. Realizing that his wife had spent their dwindling funds on these flowers, he was confused. *Why would she spend money on something we don't need?* Her reply changed Fujimura forever: "We need to feed our souls too."[16]

Fujimura's story reminds us that beauty and art are not optional add-ons to life. While our culture values productivity and efficiency, our hearts long to be delighted, craving what is good, true, and beautiful. We are made for beauty, and our souls begin to shrivel when we cease to wonder. Perhaps that's why the largest book of the Bible is a collection of poems set to music. This should not surprise us, for we are made in the image of an artist: a creative, beautiful God. In Psalm 27, after David describes God as a stronghold, one worthy of fear even amid war and attacks, he writes, "One thing have I asked of the LORD, that will I seek after: that I may dwell in the house of the LORD all the days of my life, to gaze upon the beauty of the LORD" (Ps. 27:4). God is as beautiful as he is strong, and as we dwell in his presence, we delight in his beauty.

Recapturing the Narrative

Artists played key roles in the biblical story of redemption. David was a musician. Bezalel was a designer. Solomon was a poet. And artists will continue to play key roles in the kingdom of God today. In a world stripped of transcendence, artists can help recapture the beauty and wonder of God's creation. And one of the best ways they can do so is by telling stories that reflect the various aspects of the one grand story of the kingdom of God. Screenwriter Bobette Buster is right when she says, "He who tells the best story wins."[17] That's why the greatest need for Christians today is not to critique opposing views or even to provide a deductive defense of the Christian view (although there is certainly a place for both). We need to put forth a more compelling narrative.

The Canadian philosopher Charles Taylor offers an example that reveals the power of the stories we tell. According to Taylor, most people today who hold to a secular worldview are not convinced by the *data* of science but by the *story* of science.[18] Few people are looking under the microscopes and spending time in the lab, but they have been swept into the story of human progress that science (or, rather, scientism) tells.

We are a part of a grand story, and citizens of the kingdom need to tell and retell that story in compelling ways. We need artists who tell the *whole* story, not just the happy parts. Scripture gives artists the categories to show the beauty and brutality of our world, to laud the admirable and lament the deplorable. It's only when the church understands the God-given significance of art and creativity, that the world will begin to see the truth in Gerald Manly Hopkins's poem: "The world is charged with the grandeur of God."[19]

Recovering the Church's Prophetic Voice

The prophets of the Old Testament were as creative as they were bold. Ezekiel, for example, once laid on his side for 430 days to dramatically symbolize how long God's people had been in sin. He also shaved his beard with a sword and ate a paper scroll given to him by God. The prophets were known for speaking out, addressing the people of God and the society at large, and they often did so through art, poetry, and creative displays.

The church today needs to recover its prophetic voice. We need a shift in mind-set from being a "moral majority" to being a "prophetic minority," as Russell Moore says.[20] And art is one of the best ways to communicate prophetically, speaking out against injustice and casting a vision for a better way. The kingdom of God is filled with artists who can revel in and reveal the beauty of God in a way that shines God's light and exposes the darkness.

CONCLUSION

To claim Jesus as king demands that we submit all of life to his kingship. If we submit to Jesus only in areas of our choice, then we're looking to him not as a king but as a puppet. We call him Lord but try to use him to validate our own lordship. The call of the kingdom is for God's reign to shape all of life. G. K. Chesterton captures the essence of the all-encompassing nature of God's royal grace:

> You say grace before meals.
> All right.
> But I say grace before the play and the opera,
> And grace before the concert and pantomime,
> And grace before I open a book,
> And grace before sketching, painting,
> Swimming, fencing, boxing, walking, playing, dancing;
> And grace before I dip the pen in the ink.[21]

To call Jesus our king is to entrust him with all we have. Will you give your work, your rest, your play, your meals, and your artistic gifts to him?

KINGDOM PURPOSE

FOLLOW
JESUS

*Now I begin to be a disciple. . . . Let fire and cross, flocks of
beasts, broken bones, dismemberment, come upon me, so long
as I attain to Jesus Christ.*   Ignatius of Antioch

David Brooks, a columnist for the *New York Times*, set out to
discover how people today talk about the meaning of life
and the pursuit of success. He began by evaluating graduation
speeches: "As I looked around the popular culture I kept finding
the same messages everywhere: You are special. Trust yourself.
Be true to yourself." Brooks, who is not a Christian, concludes:
"This is the gospel of self-trust."[1]

Examples of the wisdom of this age are everywhere. As Ellen
DeGeneres put it in a commencement address, "My advice to you
is to be true to yourself and everything will be fine." Celebrity
chef Mario Batali advised graduates to follow "your own truth,
expressed consistently by you." The Pulitzer Prize-winning journalist Anna Quindlen urged another audience to have the courage to "honor your character, your intellect, your inclinations,
and, yes, your soul by listening to its clean clear voice instead of
following the muddied messages of a timid world."[2]

The wisdom of the day is self-help, self-improvement, and

self-expression. The message of our culture is clear and consistent. Follow your heart. Make a name for yourself. Build your own personal kingdom.

In a world characterized by self-obsession and searching for answers within, Jesus's message is to deny yourself and follow him. This is the call of Christ, and it's also the path of change and growth. If you want to mature, you have to look beyond yourself. And who better to look to than Jesus.

Many forget that the call to follow Jesus comes within the context of the kingdom of God. This is evident in Mark's Gospel where Jesus's initial proclamation—"the kingdom of God is at hand" (1:15)—is immediately accompanied with an invitation: "follow me" (1:17). To heed the call of Christ is to follow him as king and to live in light of his kingdom. This is more than an emotional decision we make at an event. It is an adventure for all of life.

THE CALL TO DISCIPLESHIP

In the New Testament, followers of Jesus are called "Christians" three times, "believers" fifteen times, and "disciples" two hundred thirty-five times. Since the call of Christ is to be a disciple, let's make sure we understand what it means.

New Testament Language Used for Followers of Jesus

"Christian": 3x
"Believers": 15x
"Disciples": 253x

The word *disciple* was not unique to Christians in the first century. When Jesus called his followers "disciples," no one asked, "What's that?'" No, this was a common concept in the ancient world. Plato had disciples. Confucius had disciples. Jesus had disciples. Not only was disciple a common concept back then, it still is today. Everyone is a disciple of someone or something. But to truly understand what this means, we first have to de-spiritualize the word *disciple*. At the most basic level, a disciple follows someone in order to be with them, learn from them, and become like them.

Long before I was a disciple of Jesus, I was a disciple of another seemingly divine figure: Michael Jordan. Seriously. I followed MJ's every move so that I could learn from him and be like him. I had the shoes, I wore the jersey, and I sang with religious devotion that catchy song from his Nike commercial: *Like Mike, if I could be like Mike.*

I was a disciple.

And it's not just me. Every time someone copies Beyonce's latest hairstyle, they're being a disciple. Every time someone reads a book by a *New York Times* bestselling author, they're functioning as a disciple. Every time someone follows the career path of a person they look up to, they're acting like a disciple.

Let's break down each of these.

To be a disciple of Jesus means
to be with Jesus, learn from Jesus,
and become like Jesus.

Be with Jesus

The greatest thing about following Jesus is . . . Jesus! While there are many benefits that come from Christ, nothing compares with knowing Christ (Phil. 3:8). In our attempts to do great things *for* Jesus, we must never overlook the primacy of being *with* Jesus.

Far too often we appeal to the power of Jesus apart from the presence of Jesus. We expect the benefits without the commitment.

We want the healing of Christ apart from the lordship of Christ. But the minute you reduce Jesus to a means, he's no longer a savior but a stepping stool. And you're not worshiping him; you're using him. Jesus is not the means to your goal. He is the goal. Our first calling is to Christ himself—to know him, love him, and be with him. And yet, to be *with* Jesus is not a static experience.

Jesus is on the move. He's not bound by history; he's making history—with a story that's more powerful than any ink ever to dry on a page. Jesus is on a mission to seek and save the lost, to bring mercy and justice to the world, and to display the glory of God in such a way that makes the sun look like a Fourth of July sparkler. And as he goes, he says, "Follow me." Becoming a Christian is less like joining a club and more like jumping on a moving train. To commit to Christ is to commit to his mission.

To follow Jesus means to give him the lead. He sets the agenda. He's in control. He gets the final say. Christ is king, and to accept the kingship of Christ requires a simultaneous dethroning of self. To say, "Jesus is Lord," is also to say, "I am not Lord." To say "his way" means "not mine." That's why Jesus said, "If anyone would come after me, let him deny himself and take up his cross daily and follow me" (Luke 9:23).

Learn from Jesus

The term *disciple* comes from the Greek word *mathētēs*. It means "student," and it is also the root of the word *mathematics*. I find that a helpful connection, because math is something that has to be learned. Long division doesn't come naturally. Nobody figures out a square root just by growing up. We need to learn it. We have to be students. It's the same with being a disciple of Jesus. He calls us to be learners.

Learning from Jesus is not about learning information in order to pass a test; it's about learning to love. Surprisingly, genuine love doesn't come naturally to us. It's natural to look out for yourself at the expense of others. It's natural to look to God for your purposes rather than his. We have to learn how to love God and others.

Who better to learn from than Jesus? He said, "Take my yoke upon you, and learn from me" (Matt. 11:29). That's something any rabbi would have said to a group of disciples in the first century, but Jesus wasn't just any rabbi. He said things like, "You have heard that it was said. . . . But *I* say to you . . ." (Matt. 5:43–44), setting himself apart from other rabbis and even from the greatest teachers and sages of the Old Testament. Solomon was considered the wisest man the world had ever seen, yet Jesus said, "Something greater than Solomon is here" (Matt. 12:42).

To be a disciple is to learn constantly from Jesus. We learn from Christ through the Scriptures about who God is, how to grow in character, how to apply our faith to our work, and how to seek justice in a world of injustice. Jesus is our teacher, and he teaches us through his Word by the Spirit in the context of community.

Become Like Jesus

If you hang out with someone long enough, they start to rub off on you. You say things they say. You do things they do. You become more like them. So it is with Jesus. If we are with Jesus and learning from Jesus, we'll become more like him.

Jesus is our perfect example. He was the perfect friend who never bailed during difficult times. He used words to build up rather than tear down. He knew when to be firm and when to be gentle. Jesus was exemplary in the way he interacted with society, pressing against dehumanizing cultural norms and loving those who appeared unlovable.

To be a disciple of Jesus means to become more like Jesus every day in every way. God's grace transforms us from the inside out, and the Holy Spirit empowers us to overcome sin and become like our Savior.

THE CENTRALITY OF THE GOSPEL

I've been through quite a few graduation ceremonies in my life. In my youth karate class, I graduated from white belt to yellow belt (unfortunately, I never got any further). At my sixth-grade graduation, our entire class sang Michael Jackson's "Heal the World" (having conquered elementary school, we were certainly ready). Every graduation ceremony was different, but they all represented the same idea: moving on from one thing to the next.

Unfortunately, a lot of Christians think they've graduated from the gospel. We assume that the gospel is only for non-Christians or beginners. It's the entry-level basics of Christianity, the training for JV that you eventually move past when you become a varsity Christian. But this approach couldn't be further from the truth. You never graduate from the gospel. The good news of Jesus is what saves *and* sustains. The gospel is an endless well of power that we are to draw from for the rest of our lives. Tim Keller has faithfully taught this principle throughout his ministry in New York City:

> We never "get beyond the gospel" in our Christian life to something more "advanced." The gospel is not the first "step" in a "stairway" of truths, rather, it is more like the "hub" in a "wheel" of truth. The gospel is not just the A-B-C's but the A to Z of Christianity. The gospel is not just the minimum required doctrine necessary to enter the kingdom, but the way we make all progress in the kingdom.[3]

Keller was not the first to make such a claim. In fact, this is the heart of biblical Christianity, as the Reformers knew well. Five-hundred years ago, Martin Luther put it this way:

The gospel . . . is also the principal article of all Christian
doctrine, wherein the knowledge of all godliness consisteth.
Most necessary it is, therefore, that we should know this
article well, teach it unto others, and beat it into their heads
continually.[4]

This gospel-for-all-of-life principle is on display in Paul's first
letter to the church in Corinth. The young Christians in Corinth
were experiencing major (and embarrassing) problems. They
were dividing over who their favorite preacher was, some were
getting drunk during communion, and one man even hooked
up with his stepmom. But what was Paul's remedy for their sin
and disobedience? He didn't send them to a unity conference. He
didn't recommend a 12-step group for alcohol abuse. He didn't
tell them to start a sexual purity ministry. According to Paul,
the remedy they needed was the gospel. He said, "Now I would
remind you, brothers, of the gospel I preached to you, which you
received, in which you stand" (1 Cor. 15:1).

These Christians (Paul called them "brothers" in Christ)
needed to be reminded of the gospel. They already knew it, but
they were not trusting in the gospel in the moment, which is why
they were acting the way they were. They were not running to
Jesus for comfort; they were running to alcohol. They were not
uniting in their Savior; they were divided by their preferences.
They were not experiencing intimacy with Christ, so they were
finding it in sexual immorality. Paul reminded them of the gospel
because they didn't ultimately have a division problem, an alcohol problem, or a sexuality problem—they had a gospel problem.
The root problem (the sin beneath every sin) was that they did not
trust in the sufficiency of Christ's saving work. The solution for
sin is not merely trying harder but trusting in Jesus and living in
light of his life, death, and resurrection. The gospel not only saves
us from our sin; it makes us more and more like our Savior.

Paul's message to the church in Corinth and to us today is not only to receive the gospel but to stand in it (1 Cor. 15:1–2). The good news is the foundation for standing firm in a difficult and ever-changing world. Practically speaking, it gets at what motivates or drives us toward change and holiness. Many Christians are motivated by guilt and shame. "Stop sinning!" they say. "Good Christians don't sin." "God will be disappointed in you if you sin." Although shame and guilt are powerful motivators, they don't lead to health and freedom but to further bondage and shame.

Jesus changes all of this. Because of the gospel, we're motivated not by guilt but by gratitude. When I fix my eyes on Jesus and remember what he has done for me, I rejoice over his perfect life that is credited to me, his sacrificial death that removes my guilt and shame, and his victorious resurrection that gives me the power to overcome sin. As my gratitude for the gospel grows, I can walk in a manner worthy of my calling. I don't need to be enslaved to sin because I've been set free. I can say no to weaker desires because I'm saying yes to a greater desire. This doesn't rule out the need to strive for holiness; it just means that we are to strive with a grace-driven effort (Phil. 2:12–13). We do not work *for* grace but *from* grace.

For me personally, this has been a long process of learning how to apply the gospel to my life. For example, one night several years ago, I was talking with my wife and I said, "I think I have a comparison problem." I had recently been to a conference and left feeling discouraged after comparing myself to the main speakers. Like the good wife that she is, she gently started asking me questions to get beneath the surface of my statement. "What do they have that you are craving? What exactly do you envy about their position?" What emerged was my underlying belief that when I saw these people on stage, they were getting the approval I longed for in my own life. People affirmed and applauded them, and I craved that approval. My wife helped me realize that I didn't have a comparison problem. I had a *gospel* problem. There I was, longing for the approval of others, when the king of the universe already approves of me in Christ. God looks at me and sees the righteousness of Christ and says, "This is my son whom I love; with him I'm well pleased." Because God approves of me in Christ, I'm set free from living for the approval of others.

That day I could have passed a test about the gospel on paper, but I wasn't believing it in my heart. God gently and graciously reminded me of the best news ever, and that's what I need every day of my life until the Lord returns to complete the good work he began.

In the school of life, you will never graduate from the gospel or outgrow the love of God. The good news of Jesus is not only the entry point into the kingdom of God; it is the foundation for a lifetime of following the king.

THE HEART OF CHANGE

The gospel is the power for transformation. But unless the gospel grips your heart, you'll settle for the typical way that many Christians seek change: behavior modification. Let's say, for example, that you struggle with anger and find yourself lashing out at people. The behavior-modification approach focuses on external obedience apart from heart transformation. The method is simple: stop doing bad, start doing good—all driven by trying harder. Inevitably this ends up in the spin cycle of failure, guilt, trying harder, and then more failure and deeper guilt, until we reach despair or settle for duplicity.

God's way of change is not behavior modification; it is inside-out transformation. Proverbs 4:23 says that the heart is the wellspring of life. In other words, behavior is an overflow of the heart, and the way we live reflects what we love. Our behavior is like the "check engine" light on the dashboard of a car. Imagine that you're driving along, having a wonderful day, when that tiny light comes on, suggesting an ominous and expensive trip to the mechanic. But what if, to "fix the problem," you simply covered up the "check engine" light or removed the bulb and then went on with your day? The problem hasn't been dealt with, only the symptom. That's how many people seek change in their lives. They spend time tinkering with the "check engine" light of behavior while ignoring the source of the problem deeper in the heart.

When the good news of Jesus penetrates our hearts, it transforms us from the inside out. The truths of the gospel reorient and recalibrate us, forming new habits, rhythms, and patterns. We want differently and think differently, so we begin to act differently (our actions shape our desires too, as we will discuss below). Remember, the heart, in the biblical sense, is the steering wheel for all of your life. As the good news of Jesus's life, death, and resurrection changes your heart, your life is transformed as an overflow of what you believe and desire.[5]

This not only reveals a different way of change but gives a different view of God. I often hear people speak of the "God of second chances" who "wipes our sins clean and gives us a blank slate." The God of the Bible gives us more than a second chance; he gives us new hearts. In Ezekiel 36:26–27, God said, "I will give you a new heart, and a new spirit I will put within you. And I will remove the heart of stone from your flesh and give you a heart of flesh. And I will put my Spirit within you, and cause you to walk in my statutes and be careful to obey my rules." This is the promise of the new covenant that was fulfilled in Christ. So much for the "God of second chances." This is the God of new creation, the God of the gospel.

Understanding the gospel at an intellectual level alone will not bring about the change we long for and need in our lives. The last thing we need is more Christians with huge heads and shriveled hearts. The gospel renews us from within and empowers us to love God with our hearts, souls, minds, and strength.

THE POWER OF THE SPIRIT

My daughter was opening presents at her third birthday party, when the one she'd been dreaming about finally ended up in her lap. As she tore the paper off the box, she immediately knew—this is it! I can't remember what the toy was, but it had buttons that made noises and lots of flashing lights. When my daughter opened the box and pulled out the toy, none of the lights or noises were working. Tears began welling up in her eyes, and when I grabbed the box to find out why it wasn't working, I saw those three dreaded words: "Batteries not included." Who are these cruel people, and why don't they provide the power for their products?

Thankfully, the Lord is not like that. What God commands in obedience, he provides for with his power. After Jesus rose from the grave, he ascended into heaven to the right hand of the Father and sent the Holy Spirit to empower his disciples for the life and mission he had called them to.

We've talked about how following Jesus requires applying the gospel to all of life, and how that must happen from the heart. To be even more specific, it's the Holy Spirit who applies the gospel to our hearts and produces fruit in our lives.

In one of his letters, the apostle Paul made a fascinating and somewhat unusual comparison between the Holy Spirit and alcohol (Eph. 5:18–20). His point was to ask, of which will you live "under the influence"? Dr. Martyn Lloyd-Jones was well suited to explain the comparison, since before he was a pastor he was a medical doctor.[6] Lloyd-Jones noted how alcohol is a depressant. That doesn't mean it makes you sad but that it chemically depresses or slows down the activity of the brain. That's why many people turn to drinking in times of pain. The alcohol makes you less aware of your problems.

The Holy Spirit operates in the opposite way. He's not a depressant; he's a stimulant. The Spirit doesn't numb your problems.

He makes you aware of the solution in Christ. The Spirit takes what you know in your head and makes it real in your heart. He opens your eyes to the beauty of the gospel, and that vision of God's beauty is what empowers you to live to the glory of God.

Oftentimes people teach about the fruit of the Spirit as if they were commands to obey. Be kind! Be loving! Be patient! But teaching the fruit of the Spirit apart from the power of the Spirit trains people to fake it. Fruit is a by-product of the Spirit at work in our hearts. It is the Holy Spirit applying the gospel to the heart that produces fruit in the lives of Jesus's disciples. This is the power we need to follow Jesus. This is the power we need to change.

Ignatius Hazim of Syria put it beautifully:

> Without the Holy Spirit,
>> God is distant,
>> Christ is in the past,
>> the Gospel is a dead letter,
>> the Church is simple organization,
>> authority is domination,
>> mission is propaganda,
>> worship is the summoning of spirits,
>> and Christian action is the morality of slaves.[7]

But with the Holy Spirit, we have all the power we need to do all that God has commanded us to do.

God calls us to constant change in the direction of holiness. Without the Spirit, we will be exhausted from trying to do something on our own power that we can only truly do with God's power. A follower of Jesus without the power of the Spirit would be like a car without gas, a cell phone without power, or coffee without caffeine. But with the power of the Spirit, we can experience the change and holiness in our lives that we long for and that Christ promises.

THE RHYTHMS OF GRACE

We all have default settings. When someone calls us out, we get defensive. When we don't get our way, we get frustrated. When people are mean to us, we want to be mean to them. Growing in holiness requires that we change our default settings. It's not just about doing more good and less bad; we need to change our inner dispositions over time.

The word that captures what I'm talking about is *character*. Character is your inner disposition that leads you to act in certain ways. It's your default setting. It's not just what you do; it's what you're inclined to do, what comes naturally to you. Good character traits, such as humility and loyalty, are called virtues. Bad character traits, such as pride and greed, are called vices. Growing in character isn't just doing more good, it's about actually changing who you are over time by cultivating virtue. It's seeing your inner dispositions—or what you are inclined to—change to align with godly character.

The process of character formation is similar to learning to play an instrument or sport. Through practice and repetition, what at first feels unnatural eventually becomes second nature. When I first started playing basketball, dribbling with my left hand felt impossible. When I tried, it was awkward and difficult. I had to focus so much to do the simplest thing. But as I practiced through repetition, dribbling with my left hand became second nature. I could do it without even thinking about it.

Character is formed in the same way. We practice virtuous habits over and over again, and they start feeling like second nature to us, gradually changing our inner dispositions.[8] For example, our default setting is selfishness, looking out for ourselves before considering the interests of others. But when you become a Christian, you learn that selfishness is the wrong setting. You know in your head that Christ did not come to be served, but to serve others. But that "me-first" attitude is still your default setting. So when you start trying to be unselfish, it's awkward at first, and difficult. As the gospel takes root in our hearts, we also need practices through which the Holy Spirit shapes our character over time. And as we develop habits (for example, consistent rhythms of serving, tithing, and praying for others) it gradually becomes more natural to put others before ourselves. By God's grace, the Holy Spirit forms new habits of godliness in your life, and over time these can even become your new default setting.

We tend to assume that our lives are shaped most significantly by the dramatic, out-of-the-norm experiences and decisions we make. But think again of how athletic skill or musical ability is developed. Is it the result of one good practice? No, it's repeated discipline and commitment over time, driven by your passion and desire. Character development is similar. It is primarily the result of mundane, repeated, daily decisions and rhythms. David Brooks, in his book *The Road to Character*, puts it well:

> Character is a set of dispositions, desires, and habits that are slowly engraved during the struggle against your own weakness. You become more disciplined, considerate, and loving through a thousand small acts of self-control, sharing, service, friendship, and refined enjoyment. If you make disciplined, caring choices, you are slowly engraving certain tendencies into your mind.[9]

Every time you sacrifice to help someone out, you're engraving that virtuous tendency in your soul. But every time you receive something without being grateful, you're engraving that vicious tendency in your soul.

So what are the repeated practices that should shape our lives day in and day out? Many have called these "spiritual disciplines": Bible reading, prayer, meditation, fasting, tithing, solitude, and others. These are essential for growth as followers of Christ. But we need more. We also need practices in our lives that bring our spiritual growth into conversation with our day-to-day lives. We need virtue-producing habits like choosing people over technology, eating meals together, and exercising and caring for our bodies. For example, consider committing to the habit of every morning reading God's Word *before* you check your phone (for either social media or email). This simple practice not only engages you in God's Word, but it reflects a kingdom-first mentality, giving God the first word in your day. Decisions like this shape your soul and character over time.

When I was thirteen years old, my dad took me to the Grand Canyon. He explained that although the size was astounding, the canyon became what we saw that day through a long process. It took thousands of years of the Colorado River slowly carving a path through the rock, deeper and deeper in the desert. It's a beautiful picture of how God transforms our character over time. The disciplines and practices of the Christian life are less like boxes to be checked and more like a river that slowly carves a path in your soul. These channels in our heart guide the flow of our loves and our desires, producing contentment and gratitude for all that God has done for us in Christ. Spiritual discipline is not only about resisting temptation but also about reordering our joys.

SOMETHING BETTER THAN SELF-HELP

We looked earlier at the values represented in graduation speeches, noting that when people today look for direction and purpose, they look to themselves. But self-help isn't just a social fad or a section at the bookstore; it is the heart of our fallen condition.

Self-help begins with something good and right: an acknowledgment that I need help. I know that the way I'm currently doing things is broken and needs to be fixed. But from there it takes a deadly detour. If I'm the one who got myself into this mess, then why would I be the most qualified person to get myself out of it? In truth, being the source of the problem disqualifies me from being the solution.

When you get sick, you go to the doctor. When your car breaks down, you go to the mechanic. If you're spiritually sick and you've wrecked your life, why would you go to yourself to fix the problem?

Turning to self instead of God is the very nature of sin, and our individualistic culture has enhanced that temptation and even attempted to glorify it.[10] We've made idols of ourselves, and we overestimate our own wisdom, knowledge, and abilities. We believe that if we just try harder or find the right method, we'll experience a better, more fulfilling or successful life. Sadly, self-help amounts to the blind leading the blind, all by yourself. Self-help isn't that helpful after all.

So if you're trying to find yourself, then also try to be honest with yourself and admit that you need more help than you possess. This is a key first step: admitting you need someone on the outside who can step in and bring real transformation. Jesus is the one you need. Don't try to reinvent yourself. Instead, Jesus calls you to die to yourself, to agree with the truth that you do not have spiritual life in yourself and need something radical to save you. You need spiritual resurrection. You need Christ the king to make you a whole new creation.

Chapter 6

SEEK
COMMUNITY

If you want to go fast, go alone. If you want to go far, go together.

African proverb

The Museum of Broken Relationships in Los Angeles serves as a monument to humanity's longing for genuine, lasting community. Exhibits in the museum display old wedding dresses, anniversary presents, and break-up letters. One of my favorites reads: "Dear Martina, I'm still using your Netflix." Why does the museum draw crowds? Why do people flock to a place dedicated to relational pain? Why do wounds from previous relationships still sting?

Because we are hardwired for community. We long for intimacy with others, for love that lasts, for people who unite around something bigger than themselves. The songs we listen to and the movies we watch tap into the ache for intimacy that we all experience within. We identify with relational brokenness, and we long for relational wholeness. That's why we won't stop pursuing genuine relationships even if they always feel just beyond our reach. We were made for community.

Unfortunately, Western culture is not setting us up well for experiencing meaningful community. In fact, it's fair to say that we live in the most individualistic society in the history of the world.[1] Harvard Professor Robert Putnam wrote a seminal book titled *Bowling Alone*, signaling the rise of individualism and the demise of community in America.[2] To illustrate his research, Putnam shares how more people than ever are bowling, and yet participation in bowling leagues has decreased. This is representative of broader cultural trends, such as lower involvement in civic engagement and local organizations, and declining membership in churches. Individualism has been pulling on the dangling, loose thread of community life, and there's hardly anything left of the sweater.

What's frightening is that Putnam's assessment came in the year 2000, long before the rise of the personally tailored, handheld, digital world we now live in. If anything, the smartphone has accelerated our movement toward physical isolation and increased focus on ourselves. The Me Generation of the seventies has been one-upped by the Selfie Generation of today. What is especially dangerous about digital technology is that it gives us a fleeting taste of feeling connected while keeping us more isolated than ever. MIT sociologist Sherry Turkle says that our culture has gone from *Bowling Alone* to being *Alone Together*.[3] We try to satisfy the longing for relational intimacy with the shallow alternative of digital connectedness. Even with hundreds or thousands of Facebook friends, so many people still feel isolated and not known.

Substitutes will not work. We were created for more. If we are made for community, then we have to look to our Maker to learn how to truly experience community. The Bible gives a grand vision for community, but it's not easy to live out. Biblical community is not a polished stock photo of glamorous people meeting in a trendy coffee shop. Real community is messy. It's difficult. It takes time. The Bible calls it the church, the community of the king.

THE CHURCH AND THE KINGDOM

Communities exist because they are bound together by something in common. Fans build communities based on their common devotion to a team. Voters form communities based on their common political beliefs. Activists create communities around a common cause. The church is the community of those united in Christ the king. Jesus is what we have in common.

The church is meant to be filled with natural-born enemies, folks from different ethnic groups, social classes, and economic levels. Jew and Gentile, slave and free, young and old, male and female—the Bible says we are now one in Christ. And because we are all centered on Christ, we have a mutual calling to one another. The church is the community of the king.

The church and the kingdom of God are distinct but related concepts. The kingdom is God's reign through God's people over God's place. It's the goal of history and eternity. The church fits within the broader vision of the kingdom of God. The church is the redeemed people of God, gathered by the gospel and organized according to the Scriptures. One day the church will not exist as it does now in a broken and hurting world. We won't need pastors to teach God's Word, for God will speak for himself. We won't need church counseling, church discipline, or even signs such as baptism and the Lord's Supper to tangibly point to the Savior—for he will be in our presence himself. The church is a provisional reality through which God is at work in this present age but will one day give way to the kingdom of God in its fullness.

This doesn't minimize the role of the church. Quite the opposite. In a world marred by sin, God's reign is being advanced in and through the church. Remember, God reigns *through his* people, and his people are the church. The scope of God's reign is all of creation, but the focus of his reign today is *in and through* the church. The church is a preview, an outpost, and an instrument of the kingdom of God.

The Church as a Preview of the Kingdom

When I go to the theater, I love watching the previews before the movie. I still remember the preview for the last Star Wars movie. In just two minutes, they showed enough for me to grasp what the movie is about. But they did it in a compelling way that made me want to experience the movie in its fullness.

That's a perfect way to understand God's intention for the church as the community of the king. The church is meant to be a preview of the coming attraction that is the eternal kingdom of God. When the world looks at the church, it should be a glimpse into God's reign on earth as it is in heaven. They should say, "That's what it looks like when love overcomes hate." "That's how a community functions when people are treated with dignity regardless of their social status." "That's how power is used not to coerce but to serve." But not only does the church offer a glimpse; it should make us long for the fullness of the kingdom. We should want to see the full show. In other words, while we can enjoy the gifts of the kingdom now, we also need to be aware that it is only a foretaste of what God has promised in the age to come. As the Australian theologian Michael Bird says, "The Spirit-filled church is the global billboard declaring good things that God has prepared for the restoration of all things."[4]

As a child, I loved when my mom would bake cookies. As she mixed the ingredients together, I would plead with her, "Mom, can I lick the spoon?" That little taste of cookie dough on the spoon was satisfying in itself, but it also made me look forward to what was coming in fifteen minutes—warm, fresh chocolate chip cookies. In a similar way, the church gives a foretaste of the kingdom today, but it should also make us long for the day when we get to feast at the banqueting table of God's eternal kingdom.

The Church as an Outpost of the Kingdom

The United States of America has embassies in capital cities all around the world. Even though a US embassy is in another country, it still functions under the laws and government of the United States. So, for example, if I were to visit the US embassy in Honduras, I would still technically be under the authority of the American government and function by American laws even though I'm in a foreign land. The embassy is an outpost of America in the middle of another nation.

The church is meant to be an embassy of the kingdom of God. As citizens of heaven, we live in this world as ambassadors of our king, functioning under his rule and representing his kingdom. In other words, although we live in this land, our life together as God's people is an outpost that operates under the authority of Jesus. One key difference between earthly embassies and the church, however, is that we are not restricted to a physical building or a piece of property in a capital city. The church is a community of disciples scattered across the world who gather locally in different places at different times to celebrate their king and encourage one another under his rule. Wherever we go, we carry the authority of our king, living by the ways of Scripture and representing God's kingdom on earth as it is in heaven. And our heavenly citizenship doesn't make us worse citizens on earth. Quite the contrary, because we pray for heaven on earth, our citizenship above compels us to seek flourishing here below. For me personally, my allegiance is to Christ the king, and it is for that very reason that I long to see the City of Angels become more like the city of God.

The technical name for an embassy is a *mission*. I like that label because it reminds me that being a citizen of God's kingdom isn't just about status and rights, it's also about our shared mission. We are exiles in a foreign land, but as citizens of God's kingdom, we operate under his authority and represent him to the communities where we live. As the Nigerian theologian Agbonkhianmeghe Orobator says, "Jesus preached the kingdom of God as a sign of the establishment of God's definitive rule over the whole universe. The church that eventually emerged looks toward this kingdom as its representation here on earth, but it does not coincide with its meaning and reality."[5]

The Church as an Instrument of the Kingdom

The Gospels tell the story of how the kingdom of God came through the Son of God. And yet while the kingdom came through Christ, it advances through Christ's people as they are empowered by the Holy Spirit. That's exactly what we see in the book of Acts.

Acts begins with Jesus talking about the kingdom of God (Acts 1:1–3) and ends with Paul talking about the kingdom of God (Acts 28:31). In between, the kingdom advances through the church's witness to Christ the king. In Acts 1 the crucified and resurrected Messiah appears to his disciples and for forty days teaches them about the kingdom of God (Acts 1:3). When Jesus's disciples ask him about the timing of the kingdom, he redirects their attention to the mission of the kingdom: "You will be my witnesses" (Acts 1:6–8). The church does not build the kingdom of God but bears witness to it—to the gracious reign of the crucified Messiah. Christ is advancing his kingdom through the Spirit-empowered church.

The church is the instrument of the kingdom of God. We are . . .

> loved to love
> forgiven to forgive
> reconciled to reconcile
> blessed to bless

set free to set free
restored to restore
renewed to renew.

God's love is meant to come to us and through us to those around us.

Many today might be surprised that God has chosen the church as the instrument of his kingdom. It's no secret the church has had its problems, whether it's the countless scandals or the constant hypocrisy. God's selection of the church as his instrument might seem like a regrettable decision, and certainly not the best way forward in advancing his kingdom. But that decision is not up to us. Jesus chose to advance his mission through the church, not through political parties or military might. Jesus said, "I will build my church, and the gates of hell shall not prevail against it" (Matt. 16:18). Jesus advances his mission through his people, and that means our commitment to Christ is inseparable from our commitment to the church.

I've always been puzzled by Jesus telling his disciples that they would do even greater things than Jesus (John 14:12). How is that possible? How could we accomplish greater things than Jesus himself? Jesus meant that we, as a multicultural, multigenerational people would take what Christ had done and extend it far beyond its reach in the first century. The scope of Jesus's geographic work during his lifetime was limited. Jesus never went far from Israel, yet the church would spread across the world. Jesus fed thousands; his church has fed millions. Jesus proclaimed good news to crowds; the church is bringing the gospel to the nations. Jesus brought reconciliation between Jews and Greeks; the church is seeking reconciliation of every tribe and tongue. The greater work of the church is a continuation of the work of Jesus, and even our "greater things" are by his grace and for his glory.

THE MISSION OF THE CHURCH IN
THE STORY OF THE KINGDOM

What is the specific role of the church within the unfolding story of Christ's kingdom? There is a divide among Christians in answering this question. For some the mission of the church is solely to make disciples through preaching the Word and equipping the saints. This means the focus of the church is on developing a distinct community amid a broken world. For others the mission of the church is to renew the culture, bringing the reign of Christ to bear on every sphere of society. According to this approach, the church seeks to transform our cities for the glory of God.

Each of these perspectives holds much good, but I believe they present us with a false dichotomy. Certainly the mission of the church is to make disciples as a community set apart from the world. But what kind of disciples? This is the key. The church is a distinct community that makes disciples and equips those disciples to be salt and light, participating in God's work of renewal in the world.

Make Disciples

It is important to acknowledge that the mission of the church is not the exact same as the mission of God (although they are certainly related and there is much overlap). God's mission is to renew heaven and earth and unite them under the kingship of Jesus (Eph. 1:10). The church has a specific calling within that broader mission. What is that calling? Jesus left no room for doubt: "Go therefore and make disciples of all nations" (Matt. 28:19).[6]

We've already learned that to *be* a disciple means to be with Jesus, to learn from Jesus, and to become like Jesus. But how do we *make* disciples? The book of Acts answers that question in narrative form. We make disciples by witnessing to Jesus in word and deed. We point people to Christ, showing and teaching how to follow Jesus in all of life. We shine a spotlight on Jesus through proclamation and demonstration. We must proclaim the gospel and live in a way that demonstrates the implications of the gospel in every aspect of life.

Jesus said, "You will receive power when the Holy Spirit has come upon you, and you will be my witnesses" (Acts 1:8). We are given God's power for God's purposes. And his purpose is that we witness to Christ. As the Chinese theologian Simon Chan says, "The ministry of the church is an extension of the ministry of Jesus in the power of the Spirit."[7] We do not raise the kingdom from the ground up but witness that the kingdom has come to us in grace.

While the church can be involved in many things, we must focus on our mission of making disciples. We should constantly ask: What is there to do that *only* the church can do? Or, to put it another way, what *must* the church do? At the end of the day, a church should be measured by their faithfulness in preaching the gospel, making disciples, and equipping the saints for ministry. As Stanley Hauerwas and William Willimon argue, the first task of the church is to be the church.[8]

Disciples Who Participate in God's Work in the World

So the mission of the church is, strictly speaking, to make disciples. But this is where our understanding of a disciple helps to expand our understanding of mission. The mission of the church is not limited to making disciples who simply know how to pray and study the Bible. We need disciples who can represent their king in *all of life*, including the spheres in which they work, live, and play. The church is to make disciples who are salt and light in the world, who love their neighbors, who do justice, love kindness, and walk humbly with God.

The opening line of the books of Acts gives a subtle hint at how disciples participate in Christ's mission in the world. "In the first book, O Theophilus, I have dealt with all that Jesus began to do" (Acts 1:1). The "first book" refers to the Gospel of Luke, which includes numerous stories of Jesus's perfect life, sacrificial death, and victorious resurrection. And yet, according to Luke, this was simply "all that Jesus *began* to do." This means the whole book of Acts, and by implication the mission of the church, is the way in which Jesus fulfills his mission. By sending the Spirit to empower the church, Christ advances his kingdom *through* his body, his church. Jesus didn't pass a baton to the church so that he could sit back and take a break. He sent the Spirit so that the church could participate in *his* mission.

At this point it may be helpful to acknowledge a distinction between the church as an *organized institution* and the church as an *organic community*. The organized, institutional church has a clear purpose (making disciples) with structures (elders and deacons) and sacraments (baptism and the Lord's Supper), as well as practices (gathering on the Lord's Day for the preaching of the Word, corporate worship and prayer, and receiving the Lord's Supper, and then following Christ together throughout the week as they are shepherded and equipped by the leaders).

The organic community of the church shares this mission and extends it as disciples sent out into the world. Built up through the preaching of the Word, they are sent out as ambassadors of reconciliation and agents of peace. Equipped by the leaders, disciples of Christ seek to love their neighbors, serve their community through their vocations, show compassion to the poor and marginalized, and witness to the grace of God in Christ. Encouraged by one another, we are sent out to be salt and light in the spheres in which God has called us.

The church's mission to the world should not be confused with merely "making the world a better place." Our goal is not to "Westernize" the majority world or to teach indigenous communities American business practices. We are driven by God's love as a part of God's mission to witness to God's kingdom. So while we seek the common good, we do so in a way that is informed by the kingdom of God. As Miroslav Volf argues, the church is called not only to *seek* the common good but also to help *define* the common good.[9] As followers of Jesus, we witness to Christ's gracious reign in word and deed in our homes and workplaces and in the public square.

The life and mission of the church is not the same thing as the kingdom of God. But today, as we live between the resurrection and return of Christ, the church is the primary instrument God uses to reveal and realize his reign on earth as it is in heaven.

HOW COMMUNITY WORKS

The local church is incredibly ordinary and yet surprisingly radical. In fact there's nothing in history quite like it. Kingdoms have risen and fallen. Movements come and go. But the church of Jesus remains, withstanding the worst the world can throw at it, and marching on with vibrancy and purpose. If you want to make a difference in the world, you can start by getting involved in a local church. When you join a local church, you are stepping into a stream of the Lord's constant work of bringing his reign on earth as it is in heaven.

The church is not a building you go to; it's a people you go with. The church is not an event you attend; it's a mission you join. The church is not a club you sign up for; it's a family you're a part of. It's about *people*. And God most often ministers to us through his people, the church. If God wants to comfort someone, he usually does so through the comfort of one of his children. If God wants to correct someone, he usually does so through a Christian speaking the truth in love. If God wants to encourage someone, he usually gives words of encouragement for his people to share. God works through his people.

People sometimes think of community as an add-on to the Christian faith, as if individual spirituality is what it's really about, and community is merely the context for facilitating my one-on-one relationship with God. But this way of thinking veers from the path of Scripture. Our love for God and love for one another are woven together so tightly that if you pull on one thread everything unravels. We need one another just as much as we need God. And we do a disservice to people by telling them of their need for God without telling them of their need for the church. Christians shouldn't call out a sin without also offering people the grace of Christ, the hope of change, and the support of community. We were made to experience the love, safety, and support that come with genuine, biblical relationships. How can we learn to cultivate this kind of community? Here are a few ways to start.

Commit to Something Bigger Than Yourself

We live in a noncommittal culture where everyone wants to keep their options open. "If I'm tied down to one thing, then I might miss so many other things?" Plagued by an overwhelming sense of FOMO (fear of missing out), we end up not committing to much at all.

This is dangerous. If you don't commit to anything in life, then you're committing to doing nothing with your life. And if you're only committed to something as long as it's good for you, then the only thing you're really committed to is yourself. Keeping your options open all the time turns out to be another form of slavery altogether, a bondage to the latest thing that is not freeing but fleeting.

Our noncommittal culture is built on a lie. The lie is that you can be free of commitment *and* have deep meaningful community. That's not how relationships work. Take marriage, for example. My wife and I have been married for thirteen years, and when we said our vows, we were choosing to limit our options. By saying "I do" to one another, we were saying "I don't" to any other options. Every commitment requires sacrifice, and a focusing of time, energy, and resources. And yet, in marriage we're limiting our options *so that* we can experience a deeper freedom in the context of a committed relationship.

The same is true when you decide to join a church. We are called to commit to the church, and like all commitments this requires sacrifice and a focusing of our resources. We choose to covenant with *these* brothers and sisters. We choose to submit to *these* leaders. We choose to give financially to *this* community and mission. This type of commitment is very different than listening to podcasts of your favorite preacher, giving sporadically when needs arise, and trying to be a close friend to everyone in your life. In an age where digital connectedness short circuits relational depth, we need to focus our commitments, and the church is the primary place to start. The kingdom of God calls us out of our puny selfish ambitions and into something bigger than we could imagine.

One of the greatest barriers to people committing to the church today is the hypocrisy of Christians in the church or wounds they have received from a church. A quick search on social media with the hashtag #WhyIDontGoToChurch shows that many people have rejected Christ because of the way people have acted in Christ's name. Ross Douhat's *Bad Religion* documents this phenomenon, showing that the church's worst enemy is not secular atheists or violent persecutors; it's hypocritical Christians (a point repeatedly made in the New Testament).[10]

Sadly, many of the accusations are true. The church has been hypocritical. God's people often fail to represent God with love and grace. And yet the church is still the bride of Christ. It's a community of recovering sinners. So before we dismiss the church, we need to accept that we cannot disrespect the bride without also offending the groom, Jesus. The church has had its problems. But the gospel doesn't need a PR campaign or a makeover. We need a church that reflects the beauty of the gospel through a life shaped by Jesus.

Be a Contributor, Not a Consumer

When I was in high school, my family went on a cruise. I've never experienced such service and luxury! People served our food, washed our dishes, made our beds, and even entertained us. On any cruise ship, there are two groups of people. There is a small group of people who do all the work, and then there is a large group of people who are there to kick back, relax, and enjoy the ride.

Sadly, many people think the church is like a cruise ship. There's a small group of people who should do all the work, perhaps the pastors or the staff or the "super Christians." The rest are there just to enjoy the ride and, of course, to evaluate the quality of the service.

But the church is not a cruise ship; it's a battleship. On a battleship, everyone on the ship is there to work, to contribute to the mission of the ship. There are not two classes of people: those who minister and those who receive. All are engaged in the work of moving the ship in the right direction, and all play their distinctive roles in the mission they've been given.

We are all in a battle. The nations rage. The enemy attacks. The storm is swirling. In a battle like this, a cruise ship will quickly be submerged. But if we understand that we serve on a battleship under a powerful and victorious commander, we can rest assured that the battle will be won. The only question is this: Will we play our role? Will we commit to the work of Christ in and through his church?

The church in America has long been plagued by something sociologists call *consumerism*. Consumerism is a mentality that sees the world through a transactional lens and is driven by the question, "What do *I* get out of it?" When consumerism is applied to the church, it takes the form of "church shopping." We "shop" for a church where we can be "fed" by the pastors. We show up on Sundays to evaluate the performance of the paid professionals, and we make our giving decisions based on whether we think we're getting our money's worth.

Jesus did not say, "Go therefore and make consumers of all nations." He said, "Make disciples," and disciples are not consumers; they are contributors. The church is not a spiritual mall that offers goods to consumers; it's a redeemed people who are on a mission to make disciples of Jesus. At our church we like to say, "Most people come to Los Angeles to take. We're here to give." Wherever God has called you, he has put you there to contribute—to give your time, your talents, and your treasure to a work bigger than you.

Be a Good Friend

As children of God, we are brothers and sisters of one another. This image of family is an incredibly powerful way to grasp what God wants for us in Christian community. It's profound and practical. Family sticks around no matter what. Family calls you out and then helps you get through it. But family also helps out in other small but significant ways. When you're sick, your family takes care of you. Your family picks you up at the airport at 1:00 a.m. Family comes to the rescue if your car breaks down on the highway in a snowstorm. That's the kind of community the church is called to be. We are a family that is bound together not by DNA but by the blood of Christ.

Yet while everyone in the church is a brother or sister in Christ, we will still have different levels of trust and safety with individual people. We will be closer with some people than with others, and that's alright. So the church needs a robust understanding of friendship as well to truly experience healthy community. We only have so much relational capacity, and so we need to be intentional about seeking out and investing in deep, meaningful friendships.

In the twelfth century, Aelred of Rievaulx claimed there were three types of friendships, each based on different shared goals:

Carnal friendship is based on affinity or amusement.

Worldly friendship is based on usefulness.

Spiritual friendship is based on a mutual commitment to following Jesus.

Spiritual friends have a shared vision of a good and fulfilling life, and they help each other in their pursuit of such a life. Aelred proclaimed, "What statement about friendship can be more sublime, more true, more valuable than this: it has been proved that friendship must begin in Christ, continue with Christ, and be perfected by Christ."[11] We need friendships that are centered on Christ and share this common goal of life together under the rule of Christ, pursuing him together.

Displays of Grace

My church meets on Sundays right down the street from the Museum of Broken Relationships. I like to think we serve as a monument of reconciled relationships, where the healing power of God's grace restores people, relationships, and whole communities. We are full of displays of God's reconciling grace. Deep friendships. Restored marriages. Reconciled families. Like all of Christ's church, we aren't a community of perfect people. We are a community of redeemed people. We are the community of the king.

Chapter 7

PURSUE
JUSTICE

The arc of the moral universe is long, but it bends towards justice.

Martin Luther King Jr.

The rap artist Kendrick Lamar is known for his musical creativity and lyrical genius. Anyone familiar with Lamar's music, however, also knows that it is deeply thoughtful, prophetic, and spiritual. In an interview, Lamar shared about the roots of his faith and his experience in church. He recounted going to church services and hearing feel-good messages with a focus on praise, hope, and a promise of a blessing just around the corner. All of this, said Lamar, "had an emptiness about it" and felt "one sided." Looking back, Lamar reflected on why:

> I've finally figured out why I left those services feeling spiritually unsatisfied as a child. I discovered more truth. But simple truth. Our God is a loving God. Yes. He's a merciful God. Yes. But he's even more so a God of DISCIPLINE. OBEDIENCE. A JEALOUS God. . . . I feel it's my calling to share the joy of God, but with exclamation, more so, the FEAR OF GOD. The balance. Knowing the power in what he can build, and also what he can destroy.[1]

Lamar tapped into something that resonates with our culture today. We no longer accept the Santa Claus God who shows up from time to time with gifts but doesn't address the real stuff of life. The injustice of the world is too much to ignore, especially when it is constantly in front of our faces through the twenty-four-hour news cycle and always in our pockets through our phones. In a world marred with pain, Lamar is right to lament forms of Christianity that seek positive and encouraging vibes while ignoring the suffering around us.

We want a God who cares when the weak are oppressed and is willing to do something about it. And that's exactly what we find when we open the Scriptures. The God of the Bible is no sentimental deity, dispensing religious fairy dust to keep us in a good mood. The Lord is a king whose righteous character compels him to defend that which he loves.

Much of what Lamar craves is captured in the biblical concept of justice. We all long for justice. But with so much injustice in the world, it feels overwhelming:

sex trafficking
slavery
poverty
racism
educational inequality
sexism
domestic abuse
abortion
police brutality
mass incarceration
and on and on . . .

How can we possibly respond to all these injustices? What can *I* do? When it comes to justice, nobody can be an expert on every issue, but the Bible does provide wisdom to face any issue with the character and resolve that are necessary. The kingdom of God gives us the framework for pursuing justice in a world of injustice.

A KINGDOM OF JUSTICE

Justice is at the heart of the biblical vision for the kingdom. Why? Because God is a just king. Psalm 9:7 says, "The LORD sits enthroned forever; he has established his throne for justice." There is much to learn, however, in order to understand and experience the justice of God's kingdom.

Justice Is God's Agenda before It's Ours

In the face of pervasive injustice, many people today have had an awakening to the need for justice in the world. And this newfound perspective often leads to ambitious ideas: *Let's begin a movement! Let's start a nonprofit!* We may feel as if *we* came up with a new idea. But God has been passionate about justice since long before you or I felt a need to get involved. Justice is God's agenda, and we get to be a part of the work that he's doing in restoring the beautiful order of his creation.[2]

God's heart for justice is put on display in Psalm 146, which tells how the Lord "executes justice for the oppressed" (v. 7). It goes on to say:

> The LORD sets the prisoners free;
> the LORD opens the eyes of the blind.
> The LORD lifts up those who are bowed down;
> the LORD loves the righteous.
> The LORD watches over the sojourners;
> he upholds the widow and the fatherless,
> but the way of the wicked he brings to ruin.

> The LORD will reign forever,
>> your God, O Zion, to all generations. (Ps. 146:8–10)

God's reign is good news for the marginalized. In fact, throughout the Old Testament, we see God's heart for the poor, the fatherless, immigrants, and widows (Zech. 7:10). These were the most vulnerable people in society and were often taken advantage of or forgotten. But God has not forgotten them. He is the "father of the fatherless" (Ps. 68:5), the husband to the widow (Isa. 54:5), the provider for the poor (Ps. 140:12), and the refuge for the immigrant (Ps. 146:9).

This is not merely an Old Testament idea, as if God shifted his attention in the New Testament to purely spiritual matters. God is unchanging, and his concern for the downtrodden is revealed even more in the coming of Christ. In fact, Jesus was born *fatherless* (Matt. 1:18–25) into a *poor* family (Luke 2:24; 2 Cor. 8:9), he immediately became an *immigrant* (Matt. 2:13), and eventually was most likely the son of a *widow* (Mark 3:31–35). In the Old Testament, God identified with the marginalized; in the New Testament, he became one of them.

Called to Be a People of Justice

Justice is God's agenda. But *how* does God execute justice? God usually brings about justice through his justified people. The Lord is the one who watches over the sojourners, but he also commands his people to care for the sojourners (Deut. 10:18–19). The Lord upholds the widow and fatherless, and he does so through a people who care for the widow and fatherless (James 1:27). God is the advocate for the poor, and he calls his people to speak up on their behalf (Prov. 31:9). God reigns through his people.

The call to be a people of justice is proclaimed beautifully by the prophet Micah. He asks the people of God, "What does the LORD require of you . . . ?" The answer is clear:

> To do justice, and to love kindness,
>   and to walk humbly with your God. (Mic. 6:8)

Justice is not merely a suggestion or a good idea; it is a requirement from God. And this is God's word for *all* of God's people. The call to justice is not an optional add-on for a few socially minded, passionate Christians. If God is passionate about something, then indifference is not an option for us. God cares about justice, and inasmuch as he's the God of justice, we are called to be a people of justice.

The kingdom call to justice was a clear part of Christ's ministry. Jesus proclaimed "the gospel of the kingdom" (Matt. 4:23) and then immediately taught his disciples the ethics of the kingdom (Matt. 5–7). The most well-known sermon of all time, typically known as the Sermon on the Mount, is a vision of how God's people live under God's reign. In the kingdom of God, people love their enemies rather than hate them, always keep their word, and are generous to the poor. In the kingdom, God's mercy and justice are shown through a people who reflect the heart of their king. The call to justice is not simply about championing an issue, but rather embodying a kingdom.

What Is Justice?

Since the Lord is a God of justice and his people are called to be a community of justice, we need to make sure we understand what justice means. While Western society thinks of justice predominantly in legal terms, the Hebrew understanding of justice was a vision of beautiful order for all of life. For the Jewish people, justice was not merely legal, it was personal, relational, social, global, and even cosmic. The biblical understanding of justice can be understood through two key concepts: equity and order.

The Hebrew word for justice—*mishpat*—refers to treating people equitably, regardless of their race, gender, socioeconomic status, or ability to contribute to society. *Mishpat* is giving someone what they deserve, whether punishment or protection. That it is done equitably is at the heart of justice. If two people deserve the same wage, but one gets less because of their gender, this is a violation of *mishpat*. If two people deserve punishment, but one is excused because they are a part of a wealthy family, this is a violation of *mishpat*.

Proverbs 11:1 provides a tangible image of God's heart for equity: "A false balance is an abomination to the LORD, but a just weight is his delight." In ancient times people would buy and sell using a scale. For example, a seller might have a ten-pound stone that would be used to measure ten pounds of wheat. But if the seller was dishonest and greedy, he might shave some weight off the stone to sell less wheat for the same price. God abhors such violation of equity. He is a God of justice.

Justice entails equity but also order. The biblical vision of justice is not merely about maintaining order in the legal system but in the way the world works. Harvard professor Elaine Scarry observes that while beauty and justice might seem to be opposite concepts, they are actually not that different.[3] If one tries to define each, they will end up using similar words like *order*, *symmetry*, and *clarity*. That's why the English word *fair* can mean either "just" or "beautiful." One could say "that trial was fair" or "that dress was the fairest of all." God cares about justice because it's the beautiful order meant for the world that he created out of love.

Justice is a beautiful vision of equity and order in the world. *Equity* could be defined as all people getting what they deserve, whether protection or punishment. *Order* could be defined as a vision of the rightful harmony and flourishing of the world. These definitions provide us with a positive vision of justice, one which is not simply about punishing wrongdoing but also promoting that which contributes to harmony and flourishing. Living a just life entails more than avoiding breaking the law. It means seeking the very things the law is there to protect. Murder is an injustice, but justice also calls for acknowledging the dignity of all human life. Stealing is an injustice, but justice calls for generosity to those in need. Slavery is an injustice, but justice calls for pursuing and protecting freedom for all.[4]

Understanding justice in this way begins to paint a picture of what it might look like to "do justice." Even more helpful, though, is a real-life example of someone who has done this well. Martin Luther King Jr., compelled by his Christian faith and the biblical idea that all people are made in the image of God, embodied the biblical call to do justice, love kindness, and walk humbly with God. In Dr. King's book *Why We Can't Wait*, he spoke of the urgent need for justice and the way in which God's people ought to pursue it. Dr. King required every person who marched with him to sign the following pledge.

Martin Luther King's Pledge

1. Meditate daily on the teachings and life of Jesus.
2. Remember always that the nonviolent movement in Birmingham seeks justice and reconciliation—not victory.
3. Walk and talk in the manner of love, for God is love.
4. Pray daily to be used by God in order that all men might be free.
5. Sacrifice personal wishes in order that all men might be free.
6. Observe with both friend and foe the ordinary rules of courtesy.
7. Seek to perform regular service for others and for the world.
8. Refrain from the violence of fist, tongue, or heart.
9. Strive to be in good spiritual and bodily health.
10. Follow the directions of the movement and of the captain on a demonstration.[5]

Dr. King knew that Jesus is the only perfect embodiment of doing justice, loving kindness, and walking humbly with God. So he taught his followers to look to Christ as the model and means of pursuing justice today.

THE UNIQUE ETHICS OF THE KINGDOM

The idea of justice is very appealing to our culture today. It is popular to march for equality and fight against oppression. But there isn't merely one idea of justice out there, as if we all agree on what justice is and simply need to achieve it. No. We all long for justice, but whose version of justice?[6] While for many years most Americans agreed on the basic principles of right and wrong (broadly agreeing with Christian principles), today there's a new morality. According to this new ethic, tolerance is the highest virtue, and denying yourself is the unforgivable sin. This new morality isn't merely a slight adjustment to Christian ethics; it is a different framework altogether.

My wife and I recently had a couple over to our house for dinner, and the contrast of different views of justice was on full display. This couple had rejected the traditional upbringing of their conservative families and discovered the freedom of a new life. They live together but are not married, spend much of their time rescuing and adopting troubled dogs, are passionate advocates for the LGBT community, enjoy smoking marijuana, and consider themselves spiritual people, having shrines in their apartment and praying regularly to crystals. As we spent the evening getting to know one another, I was struck about halfway through the night with a realization: they think we're bad people.

I had assumed—like most past generations had in our country—that churchgoing folk like us who are married with children are viewed as moral people. But as we sat in our dining room, I could read between the lines: they saw themselves possessing the moral high ground and viewed us as immoral, narrow-minded people, whose traditional beliefs were offensive to what they believed is right and wrong. Two different understandings of justice were on the table.

It's time for Christians to own up to the fact that we have a unique ethic shaped by life under God's reign. We all want human flourishing, but we have different understandings of what that means and how to achieve it. One of the most important ways that Christians can help define and contribute to the common good is by teaching the foundational idea that all people are made in the image of God and therefore deserving of dignity and value.

HUMAN DIGNITY FROM THE WOMB TO THE TOMB

What does it look like to be a people of justice in a world of injustice? Justice entails giving people their due, whether punishment or protection. What is their due? What do all people deserve? Christians believe that all people are made in the image of God and therefore are worthy of dignity, value, and respect.

Where Dignity Comes From

When it comes to dignity, the key question is: *Why* do all people have dignity and deserve certain rights? The equality of all people might sound like an obvious, self-evident truth, but it's not. Many cultures do not believe in the equality of all people. Throughout history, and still today, many cultures determine dignity based on race, gender, socioeconomic status, the family one is born into, or how much a person contributes to society. In many Eastern cultures that believe in karma and reincarnation, if someone is born into a lower caste, it is assumed that they must deserve it because they did something bad in a former life.

Science cannot prove that all people are created equal. History does not attest to the idea that all people are created equal (Aristotle, for example, believed some were born to be slaves[7]).

Why, then, do Christians believe that all people have dignity and deserve certain rights? "In the image of God he created him, male and female he created him" (Gen. 1:27). Dignity is not something that has to be earned or achieved; it is bestowed by God as a fact of every human being. As John Perkins says, "You don't give people dignity . . . you affirm it."[8]

The dignity and equality of all people are uniquely biblical ideas.[9] If it feels self-evident to you that all people are created equal, that's probably because you live in a society shaped by the biblical view that all people are made in God's image.

Dignity for All

Scripture calls us to recognize the dignity and value of *all* human life. That's why God's heart is for the unborn (Ps. 139:13–16), those with special needs (Luke 14:12–14), immigrants (Deut. 10:17–19), orphans (Ps. 10:14), our enemies (Matt. 5:44), and the elderly (1 Tim. 5:4). In other words, we're not allowed to pick and choose whose dignity we defend. Seeking justice only for people who look like you is the greatest injustice. God gives a vision of seeking justice for all, from the womb to the tomb.

Sadly, many people today divide over whose dignity to defend. Some fight for the dignity of the unborn but don't recognize the image of God in the immigrant (and vice versa). Christians are people who see the image of God in the unborn, the mentally or physically disabled, the immigrant, the widow, the poor, the prisoner, and the elderly. Not only do we acknowledge the different facets of human brokenness, but we take notice of their connectedness. For example, half of children who age out of the foster care system become homeless. And within forty-eight hours of becoming homeless, most will be approached by a trafficker. Ninety percent will at some point become incarcerated. So if you want to address homelessness, trafficking, and mass incarceration, you have to give attention to the foster care system. All brokenness is connected.[10]

Driven by Dignity More Than Needs

Acknowledging the dignity of all people reshapes the way we think of justice and mercy. We are driven not primarily by peoples' needs but by their dignity. In other words, when I see someone sleeping on the street, I see them as an image bearer of God more than as a "homeless person." When a teenage girl gets pregnant, I do not see her and her child as problems to be dealt with, but as people to be loved. Even when someone is being cruel to me, I am called to see the image of God in them before I focus on their wrongful actions. A dignity-driven approach enables us to acknowledge people's needs without defining them by their needs.[11]

For example, when I see Steve, the man who sleeps on the sidewalk at the end of my block, I'm compelled to help him because of his dignity more than his needs. He deserves to be treated with respect, which can be shown by acknowledging his presence, looking him in the eye, and learning his story over time. The dignity of all human life reminds us that we're never merely talking about "issues"; we're talking about people, image bearers of God who are worthy of respect.

The Messiah's Mission of Justice

Most people know that Jesus came to bring love and mercy, but few recognize that he also came to bring justice. In the book of Isaiah, the Lord expresses the Messiah's mission in this way: "I have put my Spirit upon him; he will bring forth justice to the nations" (Isa. 42:1). The hope of Israel was that a messiah would come and restore the beautiful order of God's creation.

When Jesus began his ministry, he made clear that he was this Messiah who would establish justice.

> The Spirit of the Lord is upon me,
>> because he has anointed me
>> to proclaim good news to the poor.
> He has sent me to proclaim liberty to the captives
>> and recovering of sight to the blind,
>> to set at liberty those who are oppressed,
> to proclaim the year of the Lord's favor. (Luke 4:18–19)

Jesus embodied justice throughout his life. And yet Jesus would ultimately display justice in the most shocking way. He brought about justice not by punishing the wicked but by taking their place. On the cross he who was righteous and just died in the place of the wicked and cruel. The judge took the place of the judged. The just died for the unjust. Why? To make us righteous. To make us just. In God's wisdom he made a way to justify his people *and* show forth the glory of his own justice (Rom. 3:21–26).

THE GOSPEL AND SOCIAL JUSTICE

Sadly, among Christians today there is a divide between those who champion the gospel and those who fight for justice. Some Christians are passionate about social issues such as racism, mass incarceration, and poverty, but their emphasis on social action leads to an eclipse of the gospel. Others are so focused on the good news of grace that they ignore the clear call of Scripture toward justice.[12]

How should we respond to this dichotomy between the gospel and social justice? At the most basic level, we have to resist pendulum-swinging reductionism and uphold proclaiming the gospel and seeking justice because both are clearly biblical mandates. Upholding these truths, however, does not require a balancing act, but a proper relationship. In short, the gospel creates a people who seek mercy and justice. Why? Because the gospel gives us eyes to see others the way God does, and gives new hearts that motivate us to be involved in the work of justice that God is doing. The gospel gets to the heart, drawing us to God and into God's mission. The more we understand the gospel, the more we are drawn into Christ's heart for the oppressed and hurting.

The interconnectedness of the gospel and justice, although often missed today, has been upheld throughout the history of the church. Building on teachings of the Reformers and the Puritans, Tim Keller writes:

> If a person has grasped the meaning of God's grace in his heart, he will do justice. If he doesn't live justly, then he may say with his lips that he is grateful for God's grace, but in his heart he is far from him. If he doesn't care about the poor, it reveals that at best he doesn't understand the grace he has experienced, and at worst he has not really encountered the saving mercy of God. Grace should make you just.[13]

Throughout Scripture, we see that a true encounter with the grace of God leads to a sacrificial heart for the marginalized and oppressed. Doing justice is not the reason you receive grace, but it most certainly will be a result of receiving grace. Faith produces works.

In other words, the good news that we are justified by grace becomes the motivation for seeking justice for the oppressed. Seeking justice doesn't replace the gospel, but it should flow from a heart that is transformed by the gospel. The proclamation of the gospel must be accompanied with the demonstration of mercy and justice.

SO WHAT DO I DO?

Feeling overwhelmed when talking about injustice is normal. Homelessness, sex trafficking, and racism are complex and do not have easy solutions. The weight of it all can lead to paralysis. But while you may not be able to do everything, you can do something. Here are four basic action steps for being a part of the solution.

Listen

There's a time to speak and a time to listen. Sadly, Christians are better known for the former than the latter. But to be a people of justice, we must learn to listen, especially to the victims of injustice. One of the most dignifying things you can do for a person is to listen to their story and acknowledge their experience. Dietrich Bonhoeffer called this the "ministry of listening."[14] He said that when we listen to one another, we are God's ears to others. People feel known and heard by God when they are known and heard by his people.

God gave us two ears and one mouth, so our listening and speaking should be in proportion to that. If you want to be a part of holistic justice, start listening to the stories of injustice. Ask an immigrant about their experience in America. Ask a single mom what it's like in her position. Ask someone how their ethnicity informs their faith.

Learn

In our pursuit of justice, we will only advance as far as our empathy will take us. Sympathy is feeling compassion for someone who is hurting. Empathy is caring enough to enter into their pain. It means trying to understand what someone is going through from their perspective. That's why we have to be informed if we want to be involved in the work of justice.

Read books. Watch documentaries. Ask questions. Never stop learning.

There is a lot of uninformed passion in our culture today. Social media allows anyone to publish their opinions to the world, even if those ideas are undeveloped, unfiltered, and unhelpful. It's easy to get caught up in a cultural wave of moral outrage and finger-pointing when we don't really know what we're talking about and have not examined our own hearts. But to truly seek justice, we must commit to learning the complexity of issues and understanding the problem before we try to provide a solution.

Speak

After we have listened and learned, we need to speak up. Proverbs 31:8–9 says, "Open your mouth for the mute, for the rights of all who are destitute. Open your mouth, judge righteously, defend the rights of the poor and needy." We are called to be a voice for the voiceless, an advocate for the powerless, and to use our influence or platform to expose injustice and point people to grace and truth. Call out racism or sexism when you see it. Champion those who flourish in a way that leads to the flourishing of others.

When we speak up, it must not simply be to make it clear to others that we're right and they're wrong. Speaking truth is necessary, but one of the most powerful forms of truth telling is confession. On many social issues, before we bring our apologetics (defending the faith), we may need to bring our apologies (where we haven't been consistent with our own faith). The church hasn't always been faithful to Scripture in addressing racism and sexism, in its use of power, and in matters of financial integrity. Before we can be a part of the solution, we have to own up to the ways in which we've been a part of the problem. We must acknowledge the sins of our fathers (Neh. 9:2) and take responsibility to bring change today.

Act

Proverbs 21:3 says, "To do righteousness and justice is more acceptable to the LORD than sacrifice." In other words, God doesn't want your religious affection if it doesn't overflow into a life of justice. We are called to act, and that can mean many different things (beyond listening, learning, and speaking, which are powerful actions themselves): build relationships with people who don't look like you, raise awareness for overlooked-but-important issues, defend the weak, pray for the oppressed, create conversations, vote in accordance with your faith, and live in a way that shows that you are following the king who came to bring justice.

A CASE STUDY ON RACISM

It is beyond the scope of this book to apply a kingdom view of justice to every issue in our culture today. But it is helpful to see how this works on a concrete issue. Let's look at the injustice of racism, a problem that is pervasive globally and has a long and heinous history in the United States and in the church.

To begin with, let's acknowledge that Christianity was started by a Jewish peasant who didn't speak English and never left the Middle East. And while Jesus didn't have a global impact during his earthly life, he certainly had a global vision and sent his followers with a commission to make disciples of every ethnic group in the world. Over the last two thousand years, the gospel has done more to tear down cultural barriers and bring people together than any movement this world has ever seen. That's why Richard Bauckham can boldly claim that "Christianity exhibits more cultural diversity than any other religion."[15] Most religions are attached to the culture of their origin. For example, 98 percent of Hindus and Buddhists live in Asia-Pacific.[16] The movement of Jesus, however, has truly become a worldwide, multicultural phenomenon.

Global Christianity[17]

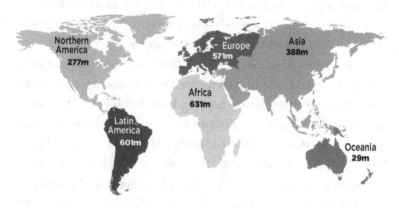

And yet, despite God's beautiful design of ethnicity and diversity, we live in a world where differences often lead to division. Racial inequity is rampant in our culture, and sadly, it's not just a dilemma for the world, it's also a problem in the church. So how can we apply the biblical vision of justice to the problem of racism? It's going to take a holistic approach, one that includes sound doctrine, compassionate community, and wise action.

The Biblical Vision of a Multiethnic Kingdom

Ethnic diversity was God's idea. Every human is made in the image of God, and the different cultures across the globe reflect the creativity of our Creator. As Scripture says, "He made from one man every nation of mankind to live on all the face of the earth" (Acts 17:26).

However, in a fallen world ethnic diversity becomes an opportunity for sinful oppression. Racism is a rejection of God's declaration that all of humanity reflects his nature. The seed of sinful hatred that was planted in the soil of human depravity has grown into a lynching tree. And while sin is first and foremost against God, our sin also leads to injustice in personal acts of racism (one person mistreating another person because of their race) and in systemic racism (patterns and sometimes laws in a culture that give advantages to particular races). We must understand that while racism is ultimately a sin problem, it is also, and derivatively, a personal, social, and political problem.

But there's good news. Jesus's death on the cross not only reconciles us to God but also reconciles us to one another. Unity and integration are possible because Jesus has severed the root of racism (sin) and torn down the dividing wall of hostility through his sacrificial death on the cross (Eph. 2:14). As the African church father Athanasius once said, "It is only on the cross that a man dies with arms outstretched . . . that He might draw His ancient people with the one and the Gentiles with the other, and join both together in himself."[18]

The gospel is the ultimate answer to racism, but it is not the sole answer to racism. We need the whole counsel of God to address racism in its personal, social, and political dimensions. Everyone is made in the image of God and worthy of dignity, value, and respect—whether they believe the gospel or not. Thus the church has a twofold calling. First, the church, as a multiethnic people united in Christ, is called to model the reconciling power of the gospel to a world longing for genuine community. Second, the church, as disciples sent out by Jesus, is called to be peacemakers and ambassadors of reconciliation in a world that is racially divided.

For a disciple of Jesus, the struggle against racism is real and can feel exhausting, but it always comes within a framework of hope. The biblical vision of a multiethnic people united in Christ is a promise before it is a command. Revelation 5 offers a glimpse of our future, with a beautiful description of Christ and his kingdom:

> You were slain, and by your blood you ransomed people for
> God from every tribe and language and people and nation,
> and you have made them a kingdom and priests to our God.
> (Rev. 5:9–10).

This is the vision of the eternal kingdom of God. As the church keeps its eyes fixed on Jesus, we have an opportunity to reflect the manifold beauty of God and the unifying power of his grace.

The Most Segregated Hour of the Week

The roots of racism go deep in the soil of American culture. The statistics and stories could stack as high as the Lincoln Memorial, and the ongoing slew of racially driven violence is sufficient evidence that Dr. King's dream has not yet been fulfilled. Recent events, however, have not created the problem but are exposing a problem that's been there all along. Though there has certainly been progress in America, we've also learned that changed laws don't automatically produce changed hearts.

The church is meant to be part of God's answer to racism in the world, but unfortunately it has often contributed to the problem instead. The old adage that Sunday morning is the most segregated hour in America sadly remains true. One study showed that while 86 percent of Protestant churches in the United States are made up of one predominant racial group, only 33 percent of American churchgoers believe that their church needs to do more in pursuing racial diversity.[19] Jerusalem, we have a problem.

As we move forward, avoiding racism is not enough. The law can prevent segregation, but love calls us to integration and unity. "Separate but equal" is not an option when we believe Christ died to bring us together. The gospel makes us a family where the waters of baptism run thicker than the blood of family origin.

Whenever Christians have been silent in the face of racism, we have failed. When Christians have been complicit in racism, we have failed. When Christians refuse to acknowledge the present reality of racism, we fail. Many in the church want to make progress, but we cannot move forward until we first acknowledge the wrongs of the past and can be honest about the pain of the present.[20] We need to listen and learn from one another, and we still have much to do.

Diverse Unity

Multicultural unity will require a deliberate pursuit shaped by wisdom, courage, sacrifice, empathy, and love. This is the responsibility of the whole church, not just a handful of passionate people, and certainly not just minorities. Racism is a sin, but so is indifference to racism. If God cares enough about bringing together every tribe and tongue that he sent his Son to the cross, then we are all called to participate in this reconciling work.

Sometimes the church has downplayed diversity for the sake of unity. People may say things like, "The color of your skin doesn't matter." But a "color blind" mentality simply shifts from taking advantage of someone's differences to ignoring their uniqueness. Different cultural backgrounds should be delighted in, not downplayed. Cesar Chavez once said, "Preservation of one's own culture does not require contempt or disrespect for other cultures."[21] In other words, when you enter into a church community, you should not have to check your cultural background at the door. Yet in many churches today that's exactly what many minorities feel the pressure to do. It is only when we embrace our diversity that we can truly be unified. To flatten our differences is to confuse unity with uniformity. Instead, we should rejoice in the richness that comes from our different backgrounds and ethnicities.

Reconciling Love

John Perkins was born to a family of sharecroppers in 1930 in Mississippi, and throughout his life he experienced explicit and extreme forms of racism. As a teenager, he witnessed a white town marshal murder his brother who had recently returned home from serving in the army. Perkins did not grow up in a religious home, and he rejected Christianity because of the racism he witnessed in the church. He saw the white church as hypocritical and the black church as a mere coping mechanism. But eventually Perkins saw the power of God's grace as he witnessed the change in the lives of people who had truly encountered Jesus. Since the day he became a follower of Jesus, Perkins has devoted his life to the pursuit of racial justice and reconciliation. "My deepest desire has been that the reconciling love that God displayed on the cross would spread into all the world, and that somehow I could participate in that mission."[22]

The pursuit of justice comes back to Jesus. It's his agenda and his mission. And yet He calls us into it. We may not all have the same impact as John Perkins, but we can all do something. We can build relationships with people who don't look like us and take time to listen to their stories and experiences. We can learn the richness of different cultural backgrounds by asking questions, visiting different cultures, and reading. We can speak up for the importance of racial equity and speak out against racism whenever it rears its ugly head. And we can take action, with wisdom and love, in making practical efforts to bring about the type of change that reflects the justice of God's kingdom.

KINGDOM PEOPLE

Chapter 8

SONS AND
DAUGHTERS

The Kingdom of God is God's love poured out on degraded humanity. It is Christ on the cross dying for the sins of the world. . . . It is men's acknowledgment of God as their Father and becoming his sons and daughters.   **Song Nai Rhee**

In 2004 a man was found beaten and bloody behind a dumpster at a Burger King in Richmond Hill, Georgia. The police found no identification on him, and upon awakening he had no memory of who he was. The hospital where he was taken already had a John Doe, so they named him after the fast-food restaurant where he was found, "BK" or "Benjaman Kyle." When no one could identify him, the media picked up the story and tried to help Benjaman discover his identity. Eventually the FBI got involved. But it was all to no avail. No one knew who he was. No fingerprints or dental records matched up with anyone in the system. For all intents and purposes, Benjaman is a man with no identity. He wakes up every morning having no idea who he is.[1]

Many Christians seem to have a similar form of gospel amnesia, waking up every day having forgotten who we are in Christ. We work tirelessly to construct our own identity through our accomplishments and well-curated social media accounts.

We believe in Jesus but forget about the new identity that we have been given by him. And despite the fact that identity is one of the most versed topics in our culture today, more people than ever are confused over who they are.

THE SEARCH FOR IDENTITY

People today feel an increasing pressure to build their own identity, yet for most of human history your identity was something given to you. You didn't decide where you lived or what you did for work. You didn't even choose who you married. Today our options are almost unlimited, but the freedom to construct our own identities comes with a pressure to earn the world's approval. What career will you choose, and how will it satisfy you and impact the world? What city will you live in, and what will that say about you? Will you marry, and how can you retain your freedom while attaching yourself to another?

Before we go too far in cultural analysis, let's personalize this. What do *you* find your identity in? Is it past failure or the hope of future success? Do you find your identity in your work or your accomplishments? Is it your personality or something you're really good at?

The search for identity is real, but most of the things we choose to build our identity on are fleeting. If you build your identity on your reputation, that can be undone with a single tweet. If you base your identity on money, an economic downturn can mean personal failure. If your identity is dependent on your career, one bad decision can bring it all crashing down.

The kingdom of God provides us with a different way of thinking about our identity. Through the gospel our identity is received, not achieved. We are drawn into a royal story, declared to be sons and daughters of the King, and sent out as ambassadors of the kingdom. God gives us an identity that's unshakable.

It doesn't depend on circumstances. It doesn't change with trends. It doesn't come and go with seasons. As we will see in the pages to come, this identity is multifaceted and rich. But at the core of our God-given identity is this profound truth: we are God's beloved children, sons and daughters of the King.

Sons and Daughters of the King

Nothing shapes your identity more than your family. As much as we tend to think we're in control of our lives, nobody chooses where they're born or what family they are born into. Your DNA is decided for you. Your parents are decided for you. This shapes your physical appearance, your personality, and those endless quirks that make you inescapably you. Even if you're not fond of your family or have distanced yourself from your parents, their influence on your life remains. Whether you are just like them or rebelling against them, they are impacting your identity.

By God's grace, however, we're drawn into a new family—one that's bound together by something stronger than our biological genes. Through the cross, God reconciles us to himself and into his family. Even though our biological family impacts our identity, our new spiritual family can have an even greater identity-shaping effect. By grace we are adopted by God, given access to God, and called to be ambassadors of God.

Adopted by the King

God created humanity in his image, and as his image bearers we are made to belong to his family. This connection between the image of God and family is made explicit in the book of Genesis. Genesis 1:26–28 tells us that all humanity is made in God's image. In Genesis 5:1–3, however, being made in the image of God is compared to a child being made in the image of their father. In other words, God created us with a family resemblance, reflecting the nature and character of our Father. We are made to be sons and daughters of the King.

Yet because of our sin we are voluntary orphans, family rebels. We have left our family, changed our legal name, and burned our old ID card. Contrary to popular belief, although all people are made in God's image, all people are not children of God. The Scriptures teach that in our sin and rebellion, we are enemies of God (Rom. 5:8). And yet God still pursues us. By the blood of Christ we can be adopted into God's family and declared to be his beloved children (Eph. 1:5). By grace God is not only your king; he is also your Father. The king of the universe is your dad.

For many people who have grown up without a father or with an abusive father, the idea of God as a father may not be appealing. In America around 40 percent of children go to bed every night without a father around, so it can be understandably difficult for them to relate to God through a title that may represent abandonment, coldness, and even abuse. This is heartbreaking, and yet there is hope because God is a father to the fatherless (Ps. 68:5).

God is everything a good father is meant to be, and more. A good father creates a relationship that encourages both intimacy and reverence. Intimacy without reverence amounts to sentimentalism. Reverence without intimacy can lead to cold submission. But intimacy *and* reverence are the way of a loving father. God requires our utmost reverence. He is strong, powerful, and mighty. And yet he offers us his unending intimacy, drawing us near to his heart in love. He is our Father, and we are adopted as his children.

Adoption not only changes our view of God, it also shapes the way we see ourselves. We are beloved children, adopted into God's royal family and given all the rights and inheritance of the king's kids. And to be clear, being adopted into the family of God does not give us a second-tier status. I have a nephew and a niece who were adopted from China, and what I knew in theory I have learned from knowing them personally—*adopted* is a verb, not an adjective. These amazing kids are not my "adopted niece and nephew," they are my niece and nephew who have been adopted into the family. As children who have been adopted into God's family, we don't receive second-tier love from God.

On the night before Jesus was betrayed, he prayed to the Father, requesting that "the love with which you have loved me may be in them" (John 17:26). This is astounding! Jesus is saying that we share in the same love that the Father has for the Son, an eternal and perfect love. We don't get leftovers of God's love or a watered-down version of his affection. Like stepping under a waterfall, we stand within the outpouring of the Father's love for the Son.

Access to the King

The more important and powerful someone is, the harder it is to get access to them. The mayor of Los Angeles is a powerful and important man, and if I tried hard enough, I might be able to get some time with him. But as we move up the political ladder to the president of the United States, an even more powerful person, I know there is no way I could get access to him. I don't have the influence, and with all his responsibilities, he wouldn't have the time for me.

God is the most important and powerful being in the universe, far more significant than any human ruler. And we might imagine that the same rules apply, that because we are insignificant God has no interest in who we are or what we do. But we would be mistaken. The Bible tells us that since we have been adopted by God, we are his children and now have unlimited access to God. We can always interrupt him. He's never too busy for us. There's no limit to the time we can spend with him.

Hebrews 4:16 says, "Let us then with confidence draw near to the throne of grace, that we may receive mercy and find grace to help in time of need." There is not a king in this world whom you or I could simply walk up to whenever we want. Only people of power, wealth, or influence are permitted to approach a human ruler or king. And even if we could approach a king, we would likely do so in fear and trembling. But we are promised limitless access to God's throne. We can enter into conversation with him freely and with full confidence that we are accepted and heard. Why? Because we know that we're approaching a "throne of grace." We know that this king rules from his throne with love and mercy.

Ambassadors of the King

God's people have a royal identity. The Bible begins with God calling humanity to rule over the earth (Gen. 1:26), and it ends with them sitting on the throne with Jesus (Rev. 3:21). In Scripture the identity of God's people as royalty is often connected with their identity as priests. They are priest-kings or a royal priesthood. This is a corporate identity for God's people that has great implications for following Jesus in our world today. To better understand how our royal and priestly identity shapes our lives as followers of Christ, let's take a closer look at how this theme unfolds in Scripture.

Adam's royal task of "edenizing" the world was coupled with a calling to "work and keep the garden" (Gen. 1:26; 2:15). While today's Western readers might miss the connotation here, an ancient Jewish reader would have recognized that these two words ("work" and "keep") are used elsewhere to describe the work of priests. Just as Adam was called to "work and keep" the garden, the priests were told to "work and keep" the temple. They were set apart to mediate the presence of God to his people. So what does this tell us about God's plan in Eden? It means that all of humanity was created by God to be a royal priesthood, mediating the blessings of God's reign to the whole world.

Adam and Eve, of course, failed to fulfill their vocation as royal priests. But God did not give up on his plan to bring his royal blessings to the end of the earth. What Adam failed to do, God called Israel to do. After he redeemed Israel from slavery in Egypt, the Lord said, "You yourselves have seen what I did to the Egyptians, and how I bore you on eagles' wings and brought you to myself. Now therefore, if you will indeed obey my voice and keep my covenant, you shall be my treasured possession among all peoples, for all the earth is mine; and you shall be to me a kingdom of priests and a holy nation" (Ex. 19:4–6).

Just as Adam and Eve failed in their calling, Israel did not fulfill their role as a royal priesthood. But Jesus, the last Adam and the faithful Israel, came as the true royal priest who would bring God's blessings to the nations. And while Jesus is the ultimate priest king, he draws his people into his own identity and mission in fulfilling his work. In Christ we are a royal priesthood as well. "You are a chosen race, a royal priesthood, a holy nation, a people for his own possession, that you may proclaim the excellencies of him who called you out of darkness into his marvelous light" (1 Peter 2:9–10).

We—as a people—have been redeemed from the kingdom of darkness and are called to shine the light of God's reign to a world in darkness.[2] That means we should be boasting about our heavenly Father.

I used to play in a basketball league in Compton, California. During one of our games I was guarding a guy who could move quicker than I can think. He was killing me on the basketball court. But even worse than getting schooled was hearing this guy's three-year-old son on the sideline yelling every time his dad would do anything good, "Oh yeah, that's my daddy!" Over and over and over again.

While it was tough for me to take, I couldn't blame the kid. He was proud of his dad. And that's the attitude that children of God should have as well. As we see God doing amazing work throughout the world and in our own communities, our hearts should scream, *Oh yeah, that's my daddy!* Every time a prayer is answered, we should tell someone, "That's my daddy!" Every time love conquers hate, we should testify, "That's my daddy!" We should boast that we are sons and daughters of the king, proclaiming his excellencies for all to hear.

We declare God's works not only with our words but with our deeds. When we comfort the hurting, the world will see that God is a comforter. When we set free the oppressed, the world will see that God is a redeemer. When we are generous to those in need, the world will see that we serve a generous God.

These are the works that characterized the church in the first few hundred years of living in a pagan world dominated by Roman power, a power often used to persecute Christians. Julian was a Roman emperor who strongly opposed Christianity, and he once said, speaking of Christians, "Nothing has so much contributed to the progress of the superstition of Christians, as their charity to strangers. . . . The impious Galileans provide not only for their own, but also for ours."[3] Even in a culture where Christians were looked down on, they shined God's light, and no one could deny their love for neighbor and stranger.

AN UNSHAKABLE IDENTITY

By grace we are sons and daughters of the king. What a glorious identity! We are part of his royal family and have a seat at his banquet table. Unlike the identities we try to build for ourselves, the identity given by God is unshakable. But to truly embrace and live in this identity, we must also understand where it comes from.

Our whole identity as Christians hangs on two small words: "in Christ."

The little phrase "in Christ" is peppered all over the New

Testament, and it is rich with meaning. But not only are you declared to be "in Christ" (2 Cor. 5:17), Scripture also says that you have "Christ in you" (Col. 1:27). Combine these two ideas and you have what theologians call the doctrine of union with Christ. It's an idea that can change your life.[4]

In Christ
+
Christ in You
=
Union with Christ

Ephesians 1:3 says that by being united with Christ, "we have every spiritual blessing." The variety of these blessings can be seen in the fact that the New Testament refers to being united with Christ over two hundred fifty times. Union with Christ is not just another doctrine to believe; it's a paradigm shift. It's a different way of understanding how we receive the immeasurable riches of God's grace. For example, most people picture receiving God's grace as if his blessings were raining down across the landscape of our lives, and we have to run around madly with a bucket trying to gather up his different blessings. There's forgiveness over here and healing over there, and I need one bucket to catch the power of the Spirit and another bucket to receive the righteousness of Christ. All kinds of blessings are available, but I have to run around trying to catch them all.

Union with Christ is a more accurate picture of how we receive the immeasurable riches of God's grace. God really is raining down all his blessings, but they aren't scattered showers forcing us to find them and collect them through our own efforts. Instead, they come to us through a single funnel, and that funnel is the person of Jesus. As long as we are with Jesus, then every spiritual blessing—redemption, forgiveness, healing, eternal life, wisdom, and everything else—comes to us through our union with Christ.

Here is why this matters. If we are united with Christ—one

with him—our identity is rooted not in what *we* can do for God, but rather in what God has done for us. If you are "in Christ," your identity is not something you have to work for or wait for, because you already are a son or daughter of the king. Ironically, it's when we stop obsessing over ourselves and start looking to Christ that we discover who we truly are.

Identity in Christ

In Christ every spiritual blessing is *already* yours.

In Christ I am the salt of the earth (Matt. 5:13).
In Christ I am the light of the world (Matt. 5:14).
In Christ I am a child of God (John 1:12).
In Christ I am declared righteous (Rom. 5:1).
In Christ I am resurrected to new life (Rom. 6:5).
In Christ I am no longer a slave to sin (Rom. 6:6).
In Christ I am dead to sin and alive to God (Rom. 6:11).
In Christ I am under no condemnation (Rom. 8:1).
In Christ I am a new creation (2 Cor. 5:17).
In Christ I am reconciled to God (2 Cor. 5:18–19).
In Christ I am a messenger of reconciliation (2 Cor. 5:19).
In Christ I am a saint (Eph. 1:1).
In Christ I am holy and blameless (Eph. 1:4).
In Christ I am adopted into the family of God (Eph. 1:5–7).
In Christ I am sealed with the Holy Spirit (Eph. 1:13).
In Christ I am free from the bondage of sin (Col. 1:13–14).
In Christ I am forgiven of my sins (Col. 1:14).
In Christ I am chosen of God, holy and beloved (Col. 3:12).
In Christ I am what I am, by God's grace (1 Cor. 15:10).

Union with Christ is the fountainhead for every blessing of God. To be "in Christ" is the foundation for an identity that cannot be shaken. If you base your identity on something that can change, your identity will be as ephemeral as the world is fleeting. In Christ you're defined not by your sin nor your success, but by your Savior, and he's unchanging. Being "in Christ" is a foundation when you are in crisis. Being "in Christ" is a constant when you are in transition. Being "in Christ" is a refuge when you are in trouble.

In Christ our identity is secure. When I feel like I'm not wanted, by faith I know that in Christ I am. I may not always feel righteous, but in Christ I am. We need faith to believe not only what is true about God but also to believe what God says is true about ourselves. If this royal identity is who we truly already are, then we no longer need to work at securing our identity but must learn how to live out of this identity.

BECOME WHO YOU ALREADY TRULY ARE

Identity is deeply connected to growth and change, but not in the way most people think. Almost every other religion in the world says that change is about becoming what you are not. If you're not pure, become pure. If you're selfish, become selfless. But Christianity says something different: *be who you already truly are in Christ.* Because our identity is given to us by faith, when God declares us righteous in Christ, we must learn who we are and then live out of that identity. In Christ you are pure, so live purely. In Christ you are light, so let your light shine. Because of grace, my identity is built not on what I do for God but on what he has done for me. Christian growth is not a matter of changing into something you are not but is about becoming who you truly are "in Christ."

Let me give an example of how this works. On August 6, 2005, at about five o'clock in the evening, I became a husband.

That was a new identity declared over me. And I've had to learn what it means to live *into* that identity. Since that day I've grown as a husband, but I am no more or less a husband now than I was then. What was true about the status of my relationship with my wife on that day is equally true today. When we place our faith in Christ, we are declared righteous, forgiven, and victorious. And then we must learn to live out of that identity. But it doesn't all happen at once. It takes time and intentionality.

There is a pattern in Scripture that is especially helpful for living out of our identity: *moral commands are based on gospel declarations.* Here are a few examples:

Forgive others because you have been forgiven (Eph. 4:32).
Love others because you have been loved (1 John 4:19).
Stop sinning because you have been freed from sin
    (Rom. 6:11–12).

This pattern is not limited to the New Testament letters, and it can even be seen in entire books of the Bible. The first half of Leviticus is about how we are made holy through atonement, and the second half is about how we are called to walk in holiness because we have been made holy. The first half of the book of Ephesians gloriously proclaims the cosmic gospel of Jesus Christ, and the second half calls us to walk in a manner worthy of the gospel. The Ten Commandments even follow this pattern. Before the list of commands of how we are to live, the Lord said, "I am the Lord your God, who brought you out of the land of Egypt, out of the house of slavery" (Ex. 20:2)—a declaration of grace, and then a call to obedience. Throughout Scripture God declares our identity over us and then calls us to live out of that identity.

This pattern reflects how I teach my own children. When they get in trouble and I need to discipline and teach them, I always remind them of two truths. First, I tell them, "I love you."

And second, I remind them, "You're my daughter." I want to see them change. I don't want them to pull out each other's hair or throw toys at the window. But my approach is not the same as the typical parenting method: "Stop that. You're being bad. I want you to be good. Try harder now." Rather, I remind them of their identity: they are beloved children. On this foundation I move on to instruction, teaching them how to function out of that identity.

I'M WITH HIM

I'll never forget my visit to the Pentagon. A friend knew someone who worked there, and on a vacation to Washington, DC, we asked if he could show us around the place. I confess I had no idea of the power and influence I was about to experience. The man giving us the tour was a three-star general in the United States Air Force. I didn't know what that meant at the time, but I quickly learned that he is one of the most powerful people in our nation, a man whose job is to oversee all the weapons acquisitions in the United States.

The three-star general met us outside the Pentagon. Passing long lines of people waiting to get inside, we walked to a special entrance. As we passed through security, the three-star general simply said, "They're with me," and they let us through. As we went through layer after layer of security, the three-star general would repeat "they're with me," and suddenly we were granted access to everything he had access to. As I heard him say, "They're with me," again and again, it became ingrained in my head. The only reason I was standing where I was standing was because of my connection to this man. "Yeah, I'm with him."

As we walked around the Pentagon, our guide was treated with the utmost respect, and because we were with him, we were treated with the utmost respect. When we went to lunch, we walked past the lounge where most people eat and went into a special room that only certain people had access too. Again, we heard the magic words: "They're with me." I'll never forget that experience. We had the access, respect, and power of a three-star general, and all because of those words, "They're with me."

God is the most powerful king in the world, and he says those powerful words to you and to me, to all who put their faith in Christ: "They're with me." And those words spoken over us start to shape our attitude and our identity. We begin to think and say to ourselves, "I'm with him." We start taking on the identity of our Father and king. We have confidence knowing that he is with us and for us. As sons and daughters of the king, our identity is unshakable and secure, and we can live into the glorious truths that have been declared over us.

Chapter 9

SOJOURNERS AND EXILES

There was an Eden on this very unhappy earth. We all long for it, and we are constantly glimpsing it: our whole nature . . . is still soaked with the sense of exile.

J. R. R. Tolkien, *The Letters of J. R. R. Tolkien*

The bell has tolled: "Christianity is in decline." Variations of this headline ran across news outlets following a survey revealing that Christianity in America has dwindled 7 percent over seven years.[1] And while the numbers are staggering, what's even more palpable is the shift in culture. It's simply not fashionable to be a Christian. Followers of Jesus are often viewed as narrow-minded bigots who are stuck in a prescientific age and will eventually die out with advancements in technology and the realization of human potential. Sadly, many churches have closed their doors in recent years, and some of those that have stayed open have caved to social pressure, lacking any distinction from the world around them.

Many Christians view this decline as a cause for concern. *Is Christianity okay? Has the kingdom become obsolete?* I think there's more to the story. We are clearly in a pivotal cultural moment right now, and there is a significant shift happening in the religious landscape. But the shift that is taking place isn't what it seems at first glance. I believe what's happening to Christianity in the West isn't an obstacle but an opportunity—an opportunity for the church to rediscover its true identity as sojourners and exiles.

DISCERNING THE CULTURAL MOMENT

Before we talk about what it means to live as sojourners and exiles, we still need to further understand the cultural milieu of our day. The common narrative, one we've been hearing for decades, is that religion belongs to the Dark Ages and is slowly fading with the dawn of human progress. As popular as this narrative has been, it is simply not true.[2] Worldwide, religion is on the rise, and Christianity in particular is thriving in unparalleled ways.[3] That's why I don't think it's accurate to say that Christianity is in decline. While it may be true in a limited sense in certain contexts, overall the kingdom of God is advancing globally in unprecedented ways. Just as Christ said it would, the kingdom has grown from humble beginnings into the greatest movement this world has ever seen (Matt. 13:31–32).

To know how to live in our world today, we need to understand what this cultural moment is all about. As we'll see, the kingdom is advancing, but it is doing so amid a world that has rejected God's reign. To be faithful as sojourners and exiles, we need to know where we are and where we're headed.

The Unprecedented Global Growth of the Kingdom of God

The so-called "decline" of Christianity is often made as a blanket statement, attempting to describe a global, historical phenomenon, but it is based on data from the Western world. Christianity, however, is not a Western religion. It is a global movement rooted in a Jewish Messiah whose kingdom spans languages, cultures, and generations. Even *if* Christianity is in decline in the West (which we will examine more closely in a moment), the global church is growing faster than it ever has before. An estimated eighty-thousand people become Christians every day throughout the world.[4] Jesus said, "I will build my church" (Matt. 16:18), and he is doing so across the earth.

In 1910 there were only 8.7 million Christians in all of Africa. Today there are 631 million Christians in Africa. In fact, one out of four Christians in the world is presently in Africa, and that number is estimated to grow to 40 percent by 2030.[5] The explosive growth of the church in China has been compared to the early church in Rome. In 1949 there were fewer than 1 million Christians in China. Today there are well over 58 million Protestants in China.[6] Still being a vast minority, these Chinese believers take their faith in Christ seriously. It is estimated that more Christian believers are found worshiping in China on any given Sunday than in the United States.[7] Nigeria has more Protestants than Germany (the birthplace of the Protestant Reformation), and Brazil has twice as many Catholics as Italy.[8] The staggering numbers could go on and on. The biblical vision of a multiethnic kingdom is being realized. The name of Jesus is being praised in 4,765 languages throughout the world.[9]

The Decline of Cultural Christianity in the West

So what about that 7 percent decline in the West? I am not convinced that Christianity is in decline in the West. *Cultural* Christianity is in decline in the West. And that's a good thing. Cultural Christianity is when people identify as Christians by name (nominally) yet faith in Christ has no real effect on their lives. While much good has been done in America for the kingdom of God, this country has also been plagued by cultural Christianity. Today 70 percent of Americans claim to be Christians, but only 36 percent are involved in a church on a weekly basis.[10]

Christianity has historically been the default religion in America. If someone believed in God and tried to be a good person, they were assumed to be a Christian. When my parents were in their twenties, for example, if they met a random person on the street, they would assume that the person was a Christian. There were cultural incentives for identifying as a Christian. Doing so would provide a person with more cultural power and enable one to be successful in more circles. Our country, for example, has never had a president who didn't at least claim to be a Christian.

So what are we to make of polls showing that Christianity has declined 7 percent in America? People who are Christians in name only (but not in any meaningful sense) are now shedding the title because it no longer helps them. It is not advantageous to be a Christian in our society anymore. In fact, with the sex and gender revolution taking place, following Jesus and the Scriptures will lead to being ostracized from social circles and losing cultural influence. It certainly seems that the days of "Christian America" are in the rearview mirror.

The End of "Christian America"

If Christian America is falling, then I say let it fall. Because it never truly was "Christian America" in the first place. There have certainly been many faithful Christians in America, but in general American Christianity has confused the kingdom of God with the American Dream, exchanged biblical doctrine with pop psychology, and replaced devotion to Jesus with vague morality. That's why many churches today emulate malls and put on services that feel like concerts. Christianity has become another commodity that I can pick and choose from to build my own kingdom and make a name for myself. "Christian America" was often a form of Christianity that ultimately existed to support me in my pursuit of individual happiness.

At its worst, "Christian America" was slave-holding, racist, consumeristic, and individualistic with a veneer of Christian spirituality over it. For Frederick Douglass, not much was "Christian" about America. The African-American abolitionist, who proclaimed the good news of Jesus and the dignity of all humanity, was himself forced into slavery. Douglass's assessment of his country's religion is devastating: "I love the pure, peaceable, and impartial Christianity of Christ; I therefore hate the corrupt, slaveholding; women-whipping, cradle-plundering, partial and hypocritical Christianity of this land."[11]

The end of "Christian America" is not an obstacle for the church; it is an opportunity to rediscover the true nature of the church as a witness to God's kingdom. We are exiles in a foreign land, and we've become far too comfortable in Western culture. America is not the promised land, and a developed Western city with artisan coffee shops and urban lofts is not the New Jerusalem. As citizens of the kingdom of heaven, we should long for the city of God as we live in the city of man. We need to learn that, as people who are devoted to Jesus, we have unique beliefs and a distinct ethic, and we shouldn't expect these to align with mainstream culture. We are exiles, and we face a moment in history when it is vital for God's people to understand their context and their role within it. The goal of the church is not to make a Christian nation but to make disciples of all nations.

WE ARE NOT HOME YET

This is not the first time God's people have found themselves in exile. Citizens of heaven have always had an identity as sojourners on earth. That's why the unfolding theme of exile in the biblical story provides a map for how to navigate our cultural context today.

In the garden of Eden, Adam and Eve were at home with God. The garden was safe. There was relational intimacy and harmony. God walked in the garden in the cool of the day. But when Adam and Eve sinned and were banished from the garden of Eden, they felt a disconnect—a deep sense that things are not the way they were meant to be. They experienced not merely physical displacement but a dissonance from living outside of God's gracious reign. The biblical word for this experience is *exile*.

Ever since that day, all of humanity has been in exile. We all are homesick for the garden of Eden and the intimacy and safety it represents. After the exile from Eden, Adam and Eve's descendants traveled east, wandering in their sin and longing to be at home with God. When God's people journeyed toward the promised land, they were called "sojourners"—a people who had a mission but not a home. Even when they made it into the promised land, they were called to care for other sojourners, because as the Lord reminded them, "you were sojourners" (Deut. 10:19).

The promised land was an Eden-like place: a land flowing with milk and honey and positioned to be a blessing to the ends of the earth. The temple was even considered the house of God (God's way of walking in the garden again). God's people were at home in God's presence. But just as Adam and Eve sinned and were sent out of the garden, Israel sinned and was exiled from the promised land. The nine hundred-mile journey to Babylon was devastating, each step a reminder that they were no longer home. Jerusalem was the city for which they had longed for generations, the city of the Great King, the place where the peace of God would be experienced but would also extend to the nations. And yet now God's people were being dragged off to a foreign land with chains around their ankles and wrists. Looking back over their shoulders at the city they loved, the smoke ascended into the sky as did their cries of lament.

After seventy years of exile in Babylon, God's people finally returned home to Israel. Yet even though they were back in the promised land, they had an ongoing sense that they remained in exile. The Old Testament ends with partial fulfillment of God's promises but an even greater longing for the fullness of the kingdom. The people returned from exile and rebuilt the temple, but the new temple was a shadow of what it was meant to be, and their experience in the land continued to resemble their exile more than the full promise of God's coming kingdom.

Echoes of exile have reverberated throughout every generation of God's people. This is why in the New Testament the apostle Peter addressed his fellow Christians as exiles scattered throughout the land (1 Peter 1:1). As citizens of the kingdom of heaven, we remain sojourners and exiles on earth. We are not home, yet.

DUAL CITIZENS

Scripture says that "our citizenship is in heaven" (Phil. 3:20). The fact that we are citizens of heaven, however, does not negate the fact that we are citizens of earth as well. We have dual citizenship: heaven and earth. That's why the apostle Paul, when he wrote to the church in Ephesus, addressed his letter to those who are "in Ephesus" and "in Christ Jesus" (Eph. 1:1). As I write this book, I am "in Christ" and "in Los Angeles." My younger brother is "in Christ" and "in Seattle." My friend Alber is "in Christ" and "in Cairo."

How do we live as dual citizens? First, we have to acknowledge that we face two ever-present temptations, each flowing from a lack of embracing the tension of our dual citizenship.

Tempted to Separate

As citizens of heaven, Christians have always been tempted to separate from the world. This temptation arises from a good biblical impulse: "Come out from them and be separate" (2 Cor. 6:17 NIV). Furthermore, the idea of separation is implicit in the call for God's people to be "holy," a word that means to be "set apart." But even though God's people have always separated from the predominant culture of our world in some sense, and that separation is rooted in a good biblical impulse, it has not always led to faithfulness to Christ.

In the New Testament, for example, the Pharisees were known for separating from those they considered unholy. In fact, the word *Pharisee* comes from the Hebrew word meaning "to separate." They sought purity for themselves and critiqued Jesus for hanging out with "sinners." In the fourth century, there was a movement of Christians who fled Rome (which had become nominally Christian) and lived in the desert to rigorously pursue holiness and communion with the Lord. One man, known as Simeon the Stylite, believed that to be truly pure he needed to separate from all people, even other Christians. When the crowds continued to flock to him because of his holiness, he found a forty-foot-tall pillar and lived at the top of it for forty years. More recently Christian fundamentalists in the United States have been defined by a separatist attitude. Maintaining the fundamentals of the faith is certainly an honorable pursuit, but this movement began to adopt a separatist posture toward the rest of the world that often leads to caring more about being right than about loving people.

Although separating from the culture may originate in a biblical impulse to be set apart for God, it confuses God's call to the church. We are not called to separate ourselves physically but to be set apart in our character and the way we live our lives. To seek holiness (being set apart) by hanging out only with other Christians and living in a bubble is contrary to the example of Jesus, who was known as a "friend of sinners" and who regularly drew near to the broken and disenfranchised. Jesus said, referring to his followers, "My prayer is not that you take them out of the world but that you protect them from the evil one" (John 17:15 NIV).

Tempted to Assimilate

As citizens of the world, living in different nations and communities, there will always be a temptation to assimilate. This also originates from a good biblical impulse, a desire to love others and become "all things to all people, that by all means I might save some" (1 Cor. 9:22). This impulse can also be taken to an extreme, resulting in a tendency to blend in and lose any distinctiveness as believers.

In the New Testament, the Sadducees tried to hold on to their religious identity while also assimilating to the reigning ideology of the day, thereby shedding doctrines such as the resurrection. In the early church, as the gospel spread throughout the Greco-Roman world, there was always a temptation to blend Christian views with Greek or Roman thinking.

This tendency to blend the faith with the patterns of the world has plagued the church throughout its history and is certainly present today. Every generation of Christians will hear the message that "times are changing, and Christianity needs to be updated to stay relevant." This mentality often results in the attempt to synchronize the Christian faith with societal norms. Think about it like this: When you sync a smart phone with a laptop, you're merging the content from two devices to create one new, shared reality. When people attempt to sync Christianity with modern culture, it also usually results in a new reality altogether that is not even recognizable as Christian.

The gospel doesn't need to be updated; it needs to be proclaimed. When the church gives into the temptation to assimilate, we sacrifice our holiness and lose our distinct identity. This happens when the church confuses the need for contextualization with adaptation. Adaptation is changing the message to tell people what they *want* to hear. Contextualization is telling people what they *need* to hear and doing so in a way they can understand and apply to life. Jesus conquered death, so following him is the one thing that will never become outdated. The greatest need for Christians today is not relevance but resilience.

LIVING IN EXILE

The Scriptures provide us with a way of being dual citizens who are faithful in exile, a pattern that avoids the extremes of separation and assimilation. In particular, Israel's time of exile in Babylon is a helpful guide for life today. When Israel was taken into exile in Babylon, they couldn't wait to get out and return home. The temptation to separate was strong. They despised Babylon. But there was also a temptation to assimilate. God's people had a poor track record of blending the unique beliefs and practices God had given to them with other religions. In fact, that's one of the reasons they were in exile in the first place, because King Solomon had synchronized his faith with pagan religions. While the Israelites longed to leave Babylon and wanted nothing to do with its people, God gave them a surprising calling.

A Call to Faithfulness

The prophet Jeremiah sent a letter to Israel in exile, with the following words from the LORD:

> Thus says the LORD of hosts, the God of Israel, to all the exiles whom I have sent into exile from Jerusalem to Babylon: Build houses and live in them; plant gardens and eat their produce. Take wives and have sons and daughters; take wives for your sons, and give your daughters in marriage, that they may bear sons and daughters; multiply there, and do not decrease. But seek the welfare of the city where I have sent you into exile, and pray to the LORD on its behalf, for in its welfare you will find your welfare. (Jer. 29:4–7)

Rather than encouraging his people to leave Babylon, God called them to settle down, build houses, start families, and seek the flourishing of the city where he had placed them. God reminds them that while Babylon had taken them captive, it was he who had sent them into exile. The sovereign Lord was calling his people to put down roots in a place that was not their home. There was no room for an "us versus them" mentality. Rather, in seeking the peace of the city, they would find their own well-being.

Just four verses later in the book of Jeremiah we read one of the most well-known verses in all of Scripture: "For I know the plans I have for you, declares the Lord, plans for welfare and not for evil, to give you a future and a hope" (Jer. 29:11). This is one of those common "life verses" that is regularly written on graduation cards coupled with a declaration that "God is going to use you to change the world." Yet many times this verse is taken out of the original context and misused. God didn't provide this promise at a graduation ceremony; he spoke it to his people in exile. Yes, he had good plans for them, but those plans included seventy years of exile where they would learn faithfulness to God in difficult circumstances. It's fine to have Jeremiah 29:11 as your life verse, as long as you're willing to be faithful to a God who may call you to suffer in exile for seventy years. That's the kind of hope God gives.

A Portrait of Faithfulness

The call to faithfulness from Jeremiah is followed by an example of faithfulness in Daniel. The primary theme of the book of Daniel is the kingdom of God, and yet the book tells the story of four young men living in exile in Babylon. Daniel and his three friends were essentially given full-ride scholarships to the University of Babylon where they were invited to study literature and history. Babylon was a pagan culture that did not worship the

Lord or respect those who did. And yet "Daniel resolved that he would not defile himself" (Dan. 1:8). Daniel and his friends chose to remain distinct in their devotion to the Lord, and when the king set up a statue of himself that all the people were required to worship, Daniel and his friends knew they would not compromise. They understood where their ultimate allegiance lay; although they were living in the culture of Babylon, they remained faithful to their God.

A DISTINCT PRESENCE

What can we learn from God's people living in exile thousands of years ago that shapes our lives as Christians today? God calls us to be a *distinct presence*. If we're not distinct, then we will have nothing unique to offer the world. If we're not present, then we'll have no impact. To truly be a people of distinct presence, we have to follow Jesus without separating or assimilating. As Miroslav Volf says, "To live as a Christian means to keep inserting a difference into a given culture without ever stepping outside that culture to do so."[12] Faithfulness in exile means to be set apart from the city while being present within the city.

Putting Down Roots

The easiest way to lose a battle is to fail to show up, and many Christians today have tried to opt out of the battle, settling for safety and security instead. This is not the way of Jesus. Christ entered into the brokenness of the world. He was born in a manger and died on a Roman cross. He was a friend of sinners who showed up to the party and sought out the lost and lowly. Jesus said, "As the Father has sent me, even so I am sending you" (John 20:21). We are sent into the world, called to be light amid the darkness.

In a world that is increasingly transient, Christians need to settle in, put down roots, and be a faithful presence over time.

That doesn't necessarily mean that everyone needs to buy a house and live in the same city for the rest of their lives. It's less about a mortgage and more about a mentality. Wherever you are, be present, let your light shine, and seek the peace of the city that God has called you to in this season of your life.

As we are in the world, let's remember that we're not just imitating Christ; we are *in* Christ. In other words, it is our union with Christ that is our framework for mission.[13] The mission of Jesus is ongoing. It's not something that we begin; it's something we join. I like to remind our church in Los Angeles that Jesus was here long before we were, and he will be here long after we are gone. Jesus doesn't arrive in a neighborhood with a trendy church plant. No, Jesus is already at work building his church, and when we arrive we participate in the work that he is already doing.

Strange to the World

The cultural shift that is taking place in America is an opportunity for the church to remember that we have a unique way of living, an uncommon set of beliefs, and a distinct approach to community—all shaped by our devotion to Jesus. What Christians believe is not normal, nor should we expect it to be. The gospel is a counterintuitive message and will sound strange to the world. We are *for* the city, but sometimes in the name of relevance or bridge building, Christians lose any distinction *from* the city. And if the church is no different than the city, then we have nothing unique to say to the city. In that case, the church is no longer a window, giving the city a glimpse of what it could be, but a mirror, simply reflecting back what is already there. Instead, the church is called to be a counterculture for the common good. The minute we lose our distinctness is the minute we have nothing to offer.

Christians today must come to terms with the fact that we live in a pluralistic society. There is no single authoritative belief system to which all people ascribe. Rather, there are a variety of beliefs and worldviews, and while that might frustrate those who long for "Christian America," it would not have surprised the Christians of the early church. The movement of Jesus emerged amid a religiously pluralist world, and in that sense, pluralism doesn't pose a new problem for the kingdom. Yet we would be wise to recognize the difference between pluralism and relativism. Pluralism acknowledges that there are many different beliefs. Relativism says that they are all equally valid and right. We can acknowledge pluralism without becoming relativists. In other words, we can accept that everyone has the right to believe whatever they want, *and* we can still have distinct and firmly held convictions.[14]

Miroslav Volf says the way forward is not to hold back our faith, nor is it to force it on others, but we should be engaged in a thoughtful and respectable way, one that is inevitably public. Christianity has never been and never should be a "private spirituality." As Volf says, "Christian faith is . . . a 'prophetic' faith that seeks to mend the world. An idle or redundant faith—a faith that does not seek to mend the world—is a seriously malfunctioning faith. . . . Faith should be active in all spheres of life: education and arts, business and politics, communication and entertainment, and more."[15] Returning to our earlier theme of the kingdom of God affecting all of life, our faith in our king is not just another aspect of life; it shapes all of life.

Results May Vary

At times our citizenship in heaven and our citizenship on earth work together harmoniously. Being a citizen of God's kingdom usually makes me a better citizen of Los Angeles (because I'm seeking the peace of the city God has called me to). For example, because God has adopted us into his family, our church is involved in foster care and adoption in our city. The organizations we work with are grateful for our willingness to help, regardless of our faith. At other times, however, our dual citizenship comes into conflict. And if our earthly city—its government or its culture—were to force or encourage its people to do something contrary to God's Word, then our citizenship in the city of God overrides our citizenship in the city of man. For example, our allegiance to God's kingdom means that we have a different view of gender and sexuality than our city has, and that will usually not be received as a gift.

In both cases, foster care and sexuality, we are driven by our allegiance to Christ. But in one case the city will celebrate us, and in the other it will criticize us. Our allegiance to God's kingdom always takes priority over and shapes our responsibility to the city of man.

Daniel and his friends are a great example of distinct presence. As citizens of God's kingdom and called to Babylon, they were set apart from within. How does Babylon respond to them? At first, with favor. They are recognized for their wisdom and rewarded with more influence and power. Sometimes when God's people are faithful, they do well in their vocation and are applauded by the world. However, praise can also quickly turn to persecution.

The king of Babylon made a decree that whenever the horn blew, all the people of Babylon were to worship a golden image set up by the king himself. If anyone refused, they would be thrown into a fiery furnace. Daniel and his friends were faithful to the Lord and, because of their devotion to God, refused to worship the image. In this instance their faithfulness led not to favor but to the furnace. As Daniel's friends awaited their death, they were mocked and even asked whether their god could deliver them from the furnace. Their response reveals their resolve: "Our God whom we serve is able to deliver us from the burning fiery furnace, and he will deliver us out of your hand, O king. But if not, be it known to you, O king, that we will not serve your gods or worship the golden image that you have set up" (Dan. 3:17–18).

Daniel and his friends were faithful. Sometimes their

faithfulness led to the world's favor and other times to the furnace. As theologian Angukali Rotokha from Bangalore, India, says, "God's people sometimes succeed and sometimes are persecuted, but God's purposes are always fulfilled."[16]

Be faithful. Results may vary.

COMING HOME

Daniel's three friends were eventually thrown in the furnace, but the story doesn't end there. When the king looked in, he was shocked at what he saw. Not only were there three men alive and walking in the fire, but a fourth figure was walking with them. Who was this heavenly figure appearing "like a son of the gods" (Dan. 3:25)? We don't know for sure, but I think it was Jesus. Regardless, this story of the furnace in exile is pointing us to an even greater act of deliverance.

Jesus left his home in heaven and became an exile for our sakes. After his birth, he was driven away from his land into a foreign country as a sojourner (Matt. 2:13–15). When Jesus went to the cross to die for our sins, he experienced the greatest exile imaginable. Shadrach, Meshach, and Abednego went into the furnace but came out unscathed. Jesus took all of the furnace's fury by bearing our sin, judgment, and even death. Jesus took the furnace of God's wrath so that we wouldn't have to.

This is why, when Jesus was on the cross, he cried out "My God, my God, why have you forsaken me?" (Mark 15:34). Jesus went into exile to bring us home to God. In doing so, Jesus wasn't only saving us from our sins but was bringing the kingdom of God. The flaming sword of Eden symbolizes the separation of exile, but the wooden cross of Golgotha represents the reconciliation of the kingdom of God. Until Christ returns, bringing heaven and earth together in the New Jerusalem, we will remain sojourners and exiles on a journey to the greater city.

Chapter 10

SAINTS AND SINNERS

We are not yet what we shall be, but we are growing toward it.

Martin Luther

J ohn Newton embodied the best and worst of humanity. As a young man in the eighteenth century, Newton was the captain of a slave ship, overseeing and profiting from the cruel dehumanization of others. After an encounter with God's amazing grace, however, Newton was a new man. Not only was he forgiven of his sin and made new by his Savior, but he then devoted his life to serving others and abolishing slavery. As Newton looked back on his life, he understood the tension between who he was and who he would be.

> I am not what I ought to be,
> I am not what I want to be,
> I am not what I hope to be in another world;
> but still I am not what I once used to be,
> and by the grace of God I am what I am.[1]

Every Christian will experience a tension between the old and new self. We are saints, made holy by the grace of God and guaranteed a future of glory. And yet our sinful nature still lingers, digging its nails into our soul with feet firmly rooted in the grave (see Rom. 8:1–11). While there's certainly a turning point of conversion, God's work of salvation is a process that takes time. As many Christians have acknowledged: by God's grace we *have been* saved from the penalty of sin, we *are being* saved from the power of sin, and we *will be* saved from the presence of sin.

We have been saved from the **PENALTY** of sin.	We are being saved from the **POWER** of sin.	We will be saved from the **PRESENCE** of sin.

As we've seen, this internal tension takes place within a broader narrative where the kingdom has "already" come but is "not yet" in its fullness. In this chapter we'll press into the way in which this tension will shape every aspect of our lives. We need hope for tomorrow, power for today, and the wisdom to walk in the tension.

HOPE FOR TOMORROW

What we believe about the future shapes how we live in the present. And while Christians sometimes get a bad rap for their beliefs about end times, we're not the only ones who believe in the end of the world. Most physicists believe that whether the world implodes or burns out, it cannot and will not exist in its current form forever. In fact, even if not focused on "the end of the world," everyone is driven by some vision of the future. The narrative of modern progress, for example, promises to culminate in a utopian society where human potential finally brings about a painless and perfect world.

According to the Scriptures, our future hope is the kingdom of God, where the end of the world turns out to be a new beginning. The Bible doesn't give us a full picture of what it will be like, but here is a glimpse:

> Then I saw a new heaven and a new earth, for the first heaven and the first earth had passed away, and the sea was no more. And I saw the holy city, new Jerusalem, coming down out of heaven from God, prepared as a bride adorned for her husband. And I heard a loud voice from the throne saying, "Behold, the dwelling place of God is with man. He will dwell with them, and they will be his people, and God himself will be with them as their God. He will wipe away every tear from their eyes, and death shall be no more, neither shall there be mourning, nor crying, nor pain anymore, for the former things have passed away."
>
> And he who was seated on the throne said, "Behold, I am making all things new." (Rev. 21:1–5)

This passage sets forth a grand vision of eternity, defined by three key features: a renewed creation, a redeemed people, and a reigning king. It's a picture of the fulfillment of the kingdom as God's reign through God's people over God's place.

A Renewed Creation

Many Christians think of the goal of salvation as leaving earth for a disembodied heaven, where we float on clouds and sing infinitely boring songs to a God who would otherwise be lonely. It's not surprising, then, that many people aren't attracted to such an idea of the afterlife. *Los Angeles Times* columnist Joel Stein writes:

> Heaven is totally overrated. It seems boring. Clouds, listening to people play the harp. It should be somewhere you can't wait to go, like a luxury hotel. Maybe blue skies and soft music were enough to keep people in line in the 17th century, but Heaven has to step it up a bit. They're basically getting by because they only have to be better than Hell.[2]

Hyperspiritual Christians, however, are not the only ones longing for a nonmaterial eternity. Most other religions portray the afterlife as a strictly spiritual existence. The ancient Greeks saw salvation as an escape from the prison of the body. Eastern religions like Buddhism and Hinduism also aim at escaping the physical realm. Islam holds out hope for a purely spiritual existence.

The Bible offers a better hope. Revelation 21 teaches that salvation is not leaving earth for heaven, it's the *renewal* of heaven and earth. The reconciling power of God's grace bring heaven and earth together, as they were meant to be. The new creation is a physical *and* spiritual place where we will eat, play, work, and love, and do so apart from the toil and pain of this sinful world. The Bible is a rescue story, but it's not about God rescuing sinners *from* a broken creation; it's about God rescuing sinners *for* a new creation.

When my older brother was a senior in high school, he bought a '69 Chevy Blazer. Its original design was glorious: a tank-like steel machine with leather seats, four-wheel drive, and a removable roof. But several decades later it was far from its primal glory. The original silver paint was now covered with rust, the transmission didn't work like it once had, and through the hole in the floorboard you could see the street passing as you drove.

My brother bought the Blazer as a renovation project to restore it to its original glory and to take it places it had never been.

That's a small picture of what God is doing on a massive scale with the entire creation. The coming of the kingdom is a renovation project where God is taking all that is falling apart from the decay of sin and making it new. The word *renovate* actually comes from the Latin word for "make new," and though the kingdom of God began in Genesis 1–2 as a building project, it is now a full-scale renovation project. The story of the Bible begins with creation (Gen. 1–2) and ends with new creation (Rev. 21–22). In between, Christ reigns from the throne, making all things new.

The new creation will be everything that Eden was meant to be. Forget about clouds and harps. The new creation is urban: streets, creativity, people, and culture. But it's also very much like the garden of old. This city, according to Revelation 22, has a river that runs through the middle of it and a tree of life bringing healing to the nations. The New Jerusalem is going to be a city like none other the world has seen—bigger than Tokyo, more creative than Los Angeles, more fashionable than London, better architecture than Chicago, and better weather than Honolulu. But take note that the city *descends* from heaven to earth. We do not build the kingdom for God, we receive the kingdom from God. The sign of Christianity is not a ladder; it's a cross. Revelation 21–22 is a preview of the answer to Jesus's prayer "Your kingdom come, your will be done, on earth as it is in heaven" (Matt. 6:10).

A Redeemed People

What makes a city great is its people. At the heart of the Bible's vision for the garden city is God's redeemed people and their relationship with God. In fact, while the features of the New Jerusalem will be mesmerizing—the gold streets, incredible food, and beautiful scenery—they will be nothing compared to the joy of the people of God dwelling in the presence of their king.

That's why Revelation 21:3 says, "Behold, God's dwelling place is now among the people." The depth of this statement can only be understood against the backdrop of God's people longing for generations to dwell in God's presence. And the way they did this throughout most of the Scriptures was by going to the temple.

In the Old Testament, the temple was the dwelling place for a holy God and the place of atonement for unholy people. There was no temple in Eden because the garden itself was a temple where God dwelt with his people unhindered by sin. After the fall, humanity's sin separated them from God and the glory of his presence. God still longed to dwell with his people, but how could a holy God dwell with an unholy people? First, he gave them the tabernacle, and as God's people journeyed in the wilderness, God dwelt with them in this tent-like sanctuary. In the promised land, God dwelt in the temple. During this time, if you wanted to be in the presence of God, you went to the temple, because it was in the temple that you could be purified of your sin and be in God's presence apart from his judgment.

The Gospel of John describes the coming of Christ by saying, "The Word became flesh and *dwelt* among us" (John 1:14). The Greek word for "dwelt" is the same word used for "tabernacle" (literally, "Jesus *tabernacled* among us"). The message is clear: Jesus is the dwelling place of God. By declaring, "Destroy this temple, and in three days I will raise it up" (John 2:19), Jesus was saying that his resurrected body would be the new temple of God, the new dwelling place where people could be in God's presence. In other words, if you want to be in God's presence today, you don't go to the temple; you go to Jesus. And through Christ we will dwell in God's presence forever. Just as there was no temple in the garden of Eden, there will be no temple in the New Jerusalem. Why? Because these places are the fulfillment of the temple— they are the dwelling of God with his royal, priestly people.[3]

Today our lives are characterized by pain and brokenness.

We live in a world with cancer, wheel chairs, oxygen tubes, and the isolation that often comes with suffering and pain. But one day Jesus will return and wipe away every tear. He will redeem his people and renew his creation. "For the earth will be filled with the knowledge of the glory of the LORD as the waters cover the sea" (Hab. 2:14).

A Reigning King

The apex of the kingdom story is the king in all his glory. Jesus is the resurrected and glorified king, enthroned over all and bringing renewal to his creation. But Revelation 5 reminds us that Christ is a different kind of king than this world has ever seen. When John hears of a lion near the throne, he turns to see in its place a slain lamb. He then hears the host of heaven erupt with praise:

> "Worthy are you to take the scroll
>> and to open its seals,
> for you were slain, and by your blood you ransomed people for God
>> from every tribe and language and people and nation,
> and you have made them a kingdom and priests to our God,
>> and they shall reign on the earth." (vv. 9–10)

The Lion of Judah laid down his life as the Lamb of God. He reigns by self-giving love, and through his sacrificial death he makes a kingdom and restores his people to their place in the kingdom.

Jesus is a king of holy love, and while he reigns with mercy, he also rules with justice. So while Christ came in grace, he will return in judgment, a judgment that seeks the peace and justice of his good creation. That's why Revelation 21:1 says, "The sea was no more." The sea, in biblical times, represented chaos and evil, and symbolically this speaks of the new creation being free of all evil and wickedness. Christ's judgment is a banishment of sin, evil, and corruption, and all as a part of his greater work of renewal.

One of my favorite parts of the days is walking into my house after work. My four young kids hug me and jump on me, and they often end up piled on top of me on our living room floor. I love it. They love when their daddy comes home.

But occasionally I will open up the door, expecting the eruption of love, only to find an eerily quiet home with no kids running toward me. Eventually one of them will emerge, head hanging low, and say something like, "Mommy said we have something we need to tell you," and they will go on to explain how they misbehaved in a major way that day. What's interesting about these two scenarios is that I—their father—am no different in my posture coming home, yet they have responded to my coming home in completely different ways. My coming home means something *different* for them depending on where they stand with me. And when Jesus returns, some people will rejoice with gratitude while others will cower in fear. Jesus will be as loving and holy as he has ever been. And he comes ultimately to save. But where *we* are with him will determine how we respond, either with joy or shame.

Hope for Tomorrow

This glorious vision of the future—a reigning king, a redeemed people, and a new creation—gives us hope for tomorrow. The biblical understanding of hope is not merely wishful thinking. When I say, "I hope there's no traffic today in Los Angeles," it's a wish rooted in doubt. "I hope it's going to be sunny today in California" is a want rooted in probability. But when we say, "I hope in God's promises," we say this with confidence rooted not in our doubts nor in any probability but in God's sovereignty. Biblical hope is not naive optimism or wishful thinking; it is an unflinching confidence in God's power to accomplish God's purposes in God's timing.

There is hope for a fallen creation because Christ is the risen king. While speaking of the resurrection, Paul says, "If in Christ we have hope in this life only, we are of all people most to be pitied" (1 Cor. 15:19). Christ's life reminds us that he is with us in suffering. His death teaches us that he can transform us through suffering. But the resurrection means that one day Christ will put an end to suffering. The risen and reigning Jesus will wipe away every tear and we will join him in the new creation in the fullness of healing and restoration. In between the resurrection of Christ and the return of Christ, we can have a confident yet patient hope in God accomplishing his plans.

One of my favorite reasons for going to Trader Joe's is the samples there. My wife and I will go with our kids, and as we shop for food, we taste all the little samples set out along the way. These samples are a glimpse of the full feast we can have when we get home and eat the meal together as a family. And as God's people wait patiently for his return, we too are getting samples, tastes of the full feast that awaits us. United to the resurrected Christ, we can experience healing, reconciliation, and peace today. But remember, it's all just a taste. One day we will be seated at the king's table in the new creation, and we will fully taste and see that the Lord is good. Until that day, we rejoice in the victories and we lament the tragedies as we follow our crucified and risen king.

POWER FOR TODAY

For most people the expression *end times* conjures up thoughts of a zombie apocalypse and an Armageddon-like battle. Many Christians think of the end times in terms of charts and timetables that lay out a sequence of events, and therefore they spend their time searching the headlines for which of the latest global leaders might be the antichrist. The Scriptures, however, provide a different way of thinking about the end times, one that is surprisingly relevant to how we live today.

Jesus says that we are already living in the end times. He makes claims like "the kingdom of God is at hand" (Mark 1:15) and "the kingdom of God is in the midst of you" (Luke 17:21)—shocking statements for a Jewish audience who associated the coming of the kingdom with the end of the world. Paul, in his letters, wrote that "the end of the ages has come" (1 Cor. 10:11). The author of Hebrews said, "Long ago, at many times and in many ways, God spoke to our fathers by the prophets, but *in these last days* he has spoken to us by his Son" (1:1–2). According to Jesus and the New Testament authors, therefore, we are currently living in the last days. Now, before you stock up on canned food and water and move to the desert, remember that while the eschaton has *already* come, it is *not yet* fully realized. In biblical terms we live in "the present evil age" (Gal. 1:4) and in "the age to come" (Luke 18:30) simultaneously.[4] Living in light of the end does not involve elaborate predictions about the exact date of the world's ending or looking for the antichrist; it means living under the gracious reign of God and taking part in the work of renewal he is doing in and through his people.

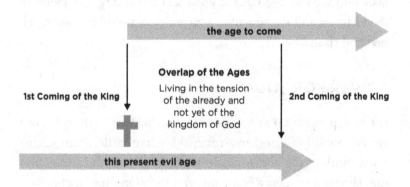

the age to come

Overlap of the Ages

1st Coming of the King

Living in the tension of the already and not yet of the kingdom of God

2nd Coming of the King

this present evil age

The end-time vision of the kingdom of God has broken into the middle of history through the gospel. The life, death, and resurrection of Jesus are the turning point of history, with all of the world hinging upon God's grace in Christ. The "end of the world" therefore began at the crucifixion. That's why when Jesus died on the cross, the sky went dark and the dead came out of tombs. These were Old Testament signs that the end of the world had arrived. God's judgment had come, with Christ absorbing it on behalf of those who have trusted in him for salvation. But while the cross is the end, it's also the beginning. The crucifixion, with the resurrection, accomplished what is necessary to reverse the curse and renew creation. The resurrection of the Son of God was the dawn of the new creation. As we await the complete renewal of the heavens and earth, everyone who is "in Christ" is declared to be a "new creation" (2 Cor. 5:17). The renewal has begun, and the reign of God is spreading, though in a hidden and subversive way.

WALKING IN THE TENSION

Though we live in the *already* and *not yet* of the kingdom of God, many Christians tend to lean toward one to the exclusion of the other. Some people stack up the Bible verses about how the kingdom has already come, and then assume that if we have enough faith we will experience the fullness of God's power today. According to this view, with enough faith we can experience prosperity in this life in every way, including health and wealth. Other people stack up the Bible verses about how the kingdom will come in the future, and then assume that the Christian life is mostly about waiting for "that day" and conserving the truth until then. This often leads to a separation from the world, a disconnect from its people and problems.

The problem with both views (besides the fact that they reduce the whole counsel of God to one stack of verses) is that they create unbiblical expectations and lead to disappointment with God. When we believe that God has only asked us to suffer and wait, we easily become bitter toward God, confused as to why he is holding out on us. If we're expecting full healing today but then are plagued with sickness and trouble, we become frustrated with God. Sadly, a lot of people are disappointed with God for breaking promises he never made. Instead, we need to align our expectations with Scripture by embracing the tension of the already and not yet of the kingdom of God.

Think of it like a set of headphones. A good set of headphones plays different sounds in each ear, helping you appreciate the fullness of a song. The left ear might have the bass and drums, while the right ear has the guitar, piano, and vocals. But the key is the way they work together, playing off one another. To follow Christ in the tension, we need to hear the already and the not yet in God's song of redemption. This is the soundtrack for a life of faithfulness, within which we should expect victory and yet not be surprised by struggle.

Expect Victory

God's gracious rule has broken into our fallen world and is bringing renewal, redemption, and restoration. We should, therefore, expect to see God's victory in our lives and in the world. Anticipate people who are far from Jesus becoming followers of Jesus. Assume that we will overcome sin in our lives. Look forward to healing of physical ailments. Plan on racial reconciliation happening in our churches. Our king is alive, and he is advancing his mission.

The greatest achievers in the history of the world all left behind unfinished work. Mozart never finished his *Requiem*. Plato's *Critias*, Tolkien's *The Silmarillion*, and Chaucer's *The Canterbury Tales* were all left undone. Da Vinci left unfinished paintings, and Michelangelo left incomplete sculptures.

Jesus finishes what he starts.

The kingdom of Christ had humble beginnings and is presently hidden beneath sacrifice and service, but one day the renewing power of Jesus will stretch to the ends of the earth. As the apostle Paul said, "I am sure of this, that he who began a good work in you will bring it to completion at the day of Jesus Christ" (Phil. 1:6). Living under God's reign means we should expect victory in this life, even amid the difficulties of this world.

Don't Be Surprised by Struggle

The kingdom has already come, but it is not yet fully realized. We should therefore not be surprised by trials, struggle, and opposition. The apostle Peter knew this well from his own life, and encouraged the church accordingly: "Beloved, do not be surprised at the fiery trial when it comes upon you to test you, as though something strange were happening to you. But rejoice insofar as you share Christ's sufferings, that you may also rejoice and be glad when his glory is revealed" (1 Peter 4:12–13). The story of the kingdom of God teaches us to not be shocked by struggle but to be prepared for it. For we serve a Messiah who brought the kingdom through the cross, and he advances his reign through the church's faithful endurance amid the brokenness of the world.

The opposition is intense, and the enemy is real. And the quickest way to lose a battle is to not realize that you're in one. Be ready. As God advances his reign, the pretender king also seeks to establish his authority. "We do not wrestle against flesh and blood, but against the rulers, against the authorities, against the cosmic powers over this present darkness, against the spiritual forces of evil in the heavenly places" (Eph. 6:12). But we must remember that the only devil we will ever face is a defeated devil. He has been disarmed of the power of accusation at the cross, and while he still prowls like a lion, his claws have been removed. Expect opposition and be ready to fight with the power of sacrificial love.

One of the ways we must deal with the struggle is by learning to lament. Because the kingdom has not yet come in its fullness, pain, grief, and brokenness are inevitable. Lamenting is a lost art in our culture today. When tragedy strikes, the default response is to point fingers and to use it as an opportunity to back up our own beliefs. Sadly, we often grab our phones and publicize our opinions through social media before we acknowledge genuine loss and grieve what has happened. The Bible offers a better first response: lament. Lament is not merely complaining, it is crying out to God from a place of honesty and authenticity. It is telling that roughly one-third of the psalms in Scripture are psalms of lament, and that we have a whole book of the Bible titled after this practice: Lamentations. Until Christ our king returns, the people of God must be a people who know how to lament.

This world offers much to enjoy, but when Jesus returns he will bring the fullness of his peace, joy, and blessings. We should therefore long for his return. Especially when the creation and its people ache and groan for renewal, we ought to pray the final prayer of Scripture: "Come, Lord Jesus." When lives are taken through another senseless shooting: "Come, Lord Jesus." When a hurricane or tsunami devastates a whole community or country: "Come, Lord Jesus." When another case of sexual abuse comes to our attention: "Come, Lord Jesus." If we truly believe what the Bible says about the eternal joy of the kingdom of God, we should be a people who yearn for the return of Christ. Even the greatest joys of this world—loving, laughing, eating, playing—are just an appetizer on the way to the banquet of God's eternal kingdom.

First John 3:2 says, "We are God's children now, *and what we will be has not yet appeared.*" Sometimes God's word to us is "not yet." And if we trust God's power and his wisdom, then we have to trust his timing. You might say, "Lord I'm ready to be married *now*," "Father, I need that job *now*," "God, I need you to deal with this difficult person *now*." But when God says "not yet" to us, he is inviting us to trust his timing and rely on his sovereignty.

To walk in the tension of the already and not yet, we need patient persistence. Patience without persistence turns into complacency. Persistence without patience results in hastiness. Patience and persistence lead to deep and lasting endurance—the kind we need to be faithful to the end.

Take Heart

Jesus gave his disciples a set of holy expectations about following him in between the already and not yet, but he also gave them hope: "In this world you will have trouble. But take heart! I have overcome the world" (John 16:33 NIV). This command to "take heart," along with its counterpart, "do not be afraid," is the most frequent command in Scripture. But while this could seem to be a general inspirational appeal, Scripture grounds this command in God's promises. We can take heart because Jesus has overcome. We don't need to fear because we have a great king. Our confidence is based not on our ability but on God's grace.

No matter what you are dealing with, no matter what you will go through, there is always hope. If death couldn't stop Jesus, then nothing can. The kingdom of God gives us a humble confidence; confident because God is accomplishing his royal purposes, and humble because we can do nothing apart from him. We can have hope because we know the end of the story. To borrow from the language of J. R. R. Tolkien: the life, death, and resurrection of Jesus mean that one day everything sad will come untrue.[5]

YOUR KINGDOM
COME

I began this book by asking how we can build our lives around what matters most. And that's the question I've sought to answer in these pages. We've learned that the place to begin is by being crystal clear about what matters most, and according to Jesus, it's the kingdom of God. Amid the worries, trials, and distractions of this world, Christ's words bring clarity and priority: "Seek first the kingdom of God" (Matt. 6:33).

We've plumbed the depths of the kingdom throughout this book, but again, the message of the kingdom can be boiled down to eight words: *God's reign through God's people over God's place.* This brief definition is more than a slogan, and it speaks of something infinitely profound. It's a vision of God bringing his loving reign to the ends of the earth and doing so through his reconciled people.

The priority of the kingdom doesn't minimize the practical realities of daily life; it puts them in perspective. The kingdom is the one thing that changes everything, including your identity, relationships, work, and purpose in life. This vision of God's all-encompassing reign gives a coherent framework for life and helps connect the dots of the Christian faith.

- The Bible is the story of the kingdom of God, giving coherence to our lives.
- Jesus is the king who brings the kingdom through his life, death, and resurrection.
- Life is infused with meaning because the kingdom offers a comprehensive perspective.
- Discipleship is about following the king in his mission of bringing the kingdom.
- The church is the community of the king, a glimpse of life under Gods' reign.
- Justice characterizes the kingdom because God is a just king.
- In Christ, we are sons and daughters of the king with an identity received by grace.
- Our citizenship in the kingdom determines and shapes our citizenship on earth.
- In between the "already" and "not yet" of the kingdom, we follow Christ in the tension.

The biblical vision of the kingdom of God is exactly what we all long for—human flourishing, global peace, and unending joy. But the comprehensive reign of God is not just something we long for; Jesus taught us to pray for it.

> Our Father in heaven,
> hallowed by your name.
> Your kingdom come,
> your will be done
>   on earth as it is in heaven. (Matt. 6:9–10)

In the narrative of the sovereign self, prayer is reduced to a good luck charm or a ritualistic way of getting what we want from God rather than encountering God himself. Prayer becomes a transaction where God is a vending machine, I pay my religious dues, and then wait for the blessing to drop.

But as Jesus teaches us, prayer is not about getting my will done in heaven; it's about God's will being done on earth. Prayer is a cry to our heavenly Father, "Your kingdom come."

Your kingdom come in my life.
Your kingdom come in my family.
Your kingdom come in our church.
Your kingdom come in our city.
Your kingdom come in this world.

Are you ready to pray this dangerous prayer? It's not a religious nicety that adds some spirituality to my otherwise well-rounded life. Prayer is an appeal to the king of the universe for his power in accordance with his purpose. We know what his purposes are, and they're not comfort, ease, and luxury. No, God's purposes are for his kingdom to come through the faithfulness of his people no matter how difficult the circumstance.

If we're honest with ourselves, the internal, silent prayer of our fallen hearts is "my kingdom come." We want God to bless our plans. We want people to follow our agenda. We want the world to praise the glory of our names. "Your kingdom come" is a dangerous prayer because we're stepping off the throne of our own lives and submitting to God's agenda of bringing restoration and renewal in creation. To pray "your kingdom come" is to ask God's gracious reign to invade the sin-corrupted spaces of our lives and our world.

What if we prayed "your kingdom come" every morning and then lived as if we believed that God would answer that prayer? What if we stopped trying to build our own kingdoms and started living for the glory of God's kingdom? What if we sought first the kingdom of God and saw everything else in our lives

through the lens of God's gracious reign? "Your kingdom come"
is a dangerous prayer. But we must pray it, for the kingdom of
God is the only hope for a world darkened by sin and pain.

In my heart, divided by sin,
let your grace prevail, bring peace within.
Reign in my soul, your will be done.
In my heart, your kingdom come.

In my life, filled with distraction,
let your mercy have its way, be my satisfaction.
Rule over my thoughts, my feelings, every one.
In my life, your kingdom come.

In our family, whatever may pass,
let your love remain, a bond that lasts.
Guide your children, conform us to your Son.
In our family, your kingdom come.

In the church, the bride of Christ so pure,
let your truth stand firm, the gospel the cure.
Lead your people, in the race to be run.
In the church, your kingdom come.

In this world, longing for restoration,
let your healing break in, the joy of the nations.
The creation groans, knowing grace will overcome.
In this world, your kingdom come.

NOTES

Chapter 1: What Matters Most

1. This quotation is commonly attributed to D. L. Moody, although like many of Moody's quotations, there is no written source because he was more of a preacher than a writer.

2. Tim Kreider, "The 'Busy' Trap," *New York Times*, June 30, 2012, https://opinionator.blogs.nytimes.com/2012/06/30/the-busy-trap/.

3. The kingdom of God is widely acknowledged as the primary theme of Jesus's preaching, and many argue that it is the unifying motif of the Old Testament, New Testament, and even the Bible as a whole. See, for example, John Bright, *The Kingdom of God: The Biblical Concept and Its Meaning for the Church* (Nashville: Abingdon, 1957), 7; and George Eldon Ladd, *The Presence of the Future: The Eschatology of Biblical Realism* (Grand Rapids: Eerdmans, 1974), xi.

4. C. S. Lewis, *Letters of C. S. Lewis*, ed. W. H. Lewis (San Diego: Harvest, 2003), 429.

5. The order of the sentence reveals the order of significance in defining God's kingdom. The kingdom is foremost about God's reign, then how he reigns through people, and then the realm of God's reign. For a more thorough overview of my definition of the kingdom of God and interaction with scholarship, see Jeremy R. Treat, *The Crucified King: Atonement and Kingdom in Biblical and Systematic Theology* (Grand Rapids: Zondervan, 2014), 40–55.

6. Although the Gospel of Matthew uses "kingdom of heaven" instead of "kingdom of God," the two phrases are mostly synonymous. Jonathan Pennington does show that Matthew's use of

"kingdom of heaven" is somewhat unique because it is part of his broader theology regarding the tension and eventual resolution between heaven and earth (Jonathan T. Pennington, *Heaven and Earth in the Gospel of Matthew*, NovTSup 126 [Boston: Brill, 2007]).

7. I alternate between the "kingdom of God" and the "kingdom of Christ" based on a Trinitarian theology of the kingdom. The kingdom breaks into history when the Father sends the Son in the power of the Spirit. In between the "already" and the "not yet," the kingdom advances as the Spirit applies the finished work of the Son so that the kingdom may be ultimately handed over to the Father.

8. Miroslav Volf, Twitter, October 7, 2015, https://twitter.com/MiroslavVolf/status/651746015368867841?ref_src=twsrc%5Etfw&ref_url=http%3A%2F%2Fbradhambrick.com%2Ftweets-of-the-week-10–14–15%2F.

Chapter 2: A Master Narrative

1. J. D. Landis, *Artist of the Beautiful: A Novel* (New York: Ballantine, 2005), back cover.

2. The philosopher Charles Taylor has shown that these so-called secular narratives are based not on the absence of belief but on a new set of beliefs. When religion is taken away, its objects of worship are not merely removed; they are replaced (Charles Taylor, *A Secular Age* [Cambridge: Belknap, 2007]).

3. At this point some readers might raise a typically postmodern concern with the idea of a metanarrative that claims to be true for all (postmodernism has been defined, after all, by Jean-Francois Lyotard as "incredulity towards metanarratives"). While much more could be said on this topic, I agree with Richard Bauckham that the biblical narrative is a "non-modern narrative" (*Bible and Mission: Christian Witness in a Postmodern World* [Grand Rapids: Baker, 2003], 90).

4. At this point I want to acknowledge that the idea of humanity being royal might sound odd or even heretical to many Christians. Is not God the only true king? Why are people being called rulers? I found myself asking the same questions years ago. When I first read *The Lion, the Witch, and the Wardrobe*

by C. S. Lewis, I thought that Lewis got the ending wrong.
I wondered, *Why do Peter, Lucy, Edmond, and Susan end up sitting
on four thrones? Aslan is the true king!* Since then, the Lord has
gently corrected me through his Word, and I now see that
Lewis was right to place the humans on the thrones.

Scripture teaches that God is king, but not only does he
reign over his people, he reigns through his people. His image
bearers are called to represent his loving reign throughout
his creation. This idea of the royalty of humanity, though first
seen in Genesis 1–2, is taught consistently throughout Scripture
(Ps. 8:3–6; 2 Tim. 2:11–12; Rev. 3:21; 22:5).

5. Ken Gnanakan, *Kingdom Concerns: A Theology of Mission Today*
   (Leicester: Inter-Varsity, 1993), 57.
6. The lineage of the seed is shown to be royal throughout the
   book of Genesis. As T. Desmond Alexander says, "This line of
   'seed' . . . is the beginning of a royal dynasty through whom
   God will bring his judgment upon the 'seed of the serpent'"
   (*The Servant King: The Bible's Portrait of the Messiah* [Vancouver:
   Regent College Press, 2003], 18).
7. Tupac Shakur, *The Rose That Grew from Concrete* (New York:
   MTV Books, 2009).
8. The following chart shows more of how the theme of the
   kingdom unfolds in the story of Scripture:

	Creation	Fall	Old Testament	New Testament	New Creation
God's Reign	Word	Judgment	Covenant	New Covenant	Presence
God's People	Adam/ Eve	None	Israel	Church	Every Tribe
God's place	Eden	Heaven	Temple	Christ	Heaven and Earth

Chapter 3: An Unmatchable King

1. Quoted in James Gibbons, *Our Christian Heritage* (John Murphy
   and Company, 1889), 238.

2. Quoted in Uri Avnery, "Soros' Sorrows: A Hungarian Kingdom
   without a King and an Admiral without a Fleet," Organized
   Rage, www.organizedrage.com/2017/07/soros-sorrows
   -hungarian-kingdom-without.html.
3. Much of this way of thinking about the kingdom of God can
   be traced back to the social gospel movement in the 1930s.
   Theologians such as Walter Rauschenbusch used the kingdom
   as a way of talking about meeting social needs while at the
   same time either refuting or minimizing the sovereignty of
   God, the sin of humanity, and the cross of Christ. H. Richard
   Niebuhr's assessment of this theology is fitting: "A God without
   wrath brought men without sin into a kingdom without
   judgment through the ministrations of a Christ without a cross"
   (*The Kingdom of God in America* [New York: Harper & Row, 1937],
   197). Unfortunately, many conservative Christians overreacted
   to the social gospel by either minimizing the importance of
   the kingdom of God and/or by belittling the social aspects of
   Christianity. As will be evident throughout this book, I don't
   believe that social justice is the gospel, but it is a necessary
   implication of the gospel.
4. *Messiah* literally means "anointed one." In the Old Testament,
   kings, priests, and prophets were anointed by oil, signifying the
   Spirit of God coming upon them to fulfill their God-given task.
   As the Messiah, Jesus is the fulfillment of Israel's longing for a
   mediator who could fully restore God's people and renew God's
   creation. The threefold office of prophet, priest, and king is
   fulfilled by Christ. Jesus is the true king who reigns on behalf
   of God, the true priest who reconciles sinners to God, and the
   true prophet who reveals the character of God.
5. In terms of defining the gospel, many focus either on Jesus's
   "gospel of the kingdom" (Matt. 4:23) or Paul's gospel of Christ's
   death and resurrection (1 Cor. 15:3–4). We obviously don't
   need to choose between Jesus and Paul, because they're both
   showing different aspects of the one gloriously multifaceted
   gospel of grace. While the kingdom is the eschatological goal
   of redemptive history, the death and resurrection of Jesus are

the glorious means and eternal foundation for that kingdom. Within a multifaceted understanding of the gospel, I offer the following summative definition: The gospel is the good news of Jesus Christ—that through his life, death, and resurrection, God has reconciled sinners and established his kingdom on earth as it is in heaven.

6. Lesslie Newbigin, *Sign of the Kingdom* (Grand Rapids: Eerdmans, 1981), 18.
7. As the second-century theologian Origen said, Jesus is the *autobasileia*—the "kingdom himself."
8. Victor Babajide Cole, "Mark," in *Africa Bible Commentary*, ed. Tokunboh Adeyemo (Grand Rapids: Zondervan, 2010), 1200.
9. Prabo Mihindukulasuriya, "How Jesus Inaugurated the Kingdom on the Cross: A Kingdom Perspective of the Atonement," *Evangelical Review of Theology* 38 (2014): 197.
10. For further reading on the doctrine of the atonement, I recommend Athanasius, *On the Incarnation* (Crestwood, NY: St. Vladimir's Seminary Press, 2002); John Stott, *The Cross of Christ* (Downers Grove, IL: InterVarsity Press, 1986); Graham Cole, *God the Peacemaker: How Atonement Brings Shalom*, New Studies in Biblical Theology (Downers Grove, IL: InterVarsity Press, 2009).
11. The Epistle to Diognetus 9:2–5, in *The Apostolic Fathers*, trans. Michael W. Holmes (Grand Rapids: Baker, 2007), 709–10.
12. Dietrich Bonhoeffer, *God Is on the Cross: Reflections on Lent and Easter* (Louisville: Westminster John Knox, 2012), 69.
13. Martin Luther King Jr., *Strength to Love* (Minneapolis: Fortress, 2010), 19.
14. Leonardo Boff, *The Way of the Cross: Way of Justice* (Maryknoll, NY: Orbis, 1980), 126.

Chapter 4: The Majestic in the Mundane

1. Stephen Hawking and Leonard Mlodinow, *The Grand Design*, repr. ed. (New York: Bantam, 2012), 8.
2. From an interview with Ken Campbell in the documentary "Beyond Our Ken," *Reality on the Rocks*, September 26, 1995 (Windfall Films).

3. René Padilla, *Mission between the Times: Essays on the Kingdom* (Grand Rapids: Eerdmans, 1985), 198.

4. Although this quote is commonly attributed to Augustine, the source is unknown. Augustine said something very similar in Contra Faustum, book 17: "For to believe what you please, and not to believe what you please, is to believe yourselves, and not the gospel."

5. Irenaeus, *Against Heresies*, trans. A. Roberts and W. H. Rambaut, *Ante-Nicene Fathers* 1 (Buffalo, NY: Christian Literature, 1885; repr., Grand Rapids: Eerdmans, 1975), 3.18.1.

6. Abraham Kuyper, "Sphere Sovereignty," in *Abraham Kuyper: A Centennial Reader*, ed. James Bratt (Grand Rapids: Eerdmans, 1998), 488.

7. Martin Luther, *Luther's Works* (St. Louis: Concordia, 1968), 14:114.

8. Amy L. Sherman, *Kingdom Calling: Vocational Stewardship for the Common Good* (Downers Grove, IL: IVP, 2011), 103–4.

9. Frederick Buechner, *Wishful Thinking: A Theological ABC* (New York: Harper & Row, 1973), 95.

10. Augustine, *The Confessions of Saint Augustine*, trans. John K. Ryan (New York: Doubleday, 1960), 43.

11. To play is to creatively enjoy something for its own good (as opposed to being productive for a greater purpose). Play becomes a game when rules are added and teams are formed (in some cases). Sport, then, is when the rules of a game are universalized and the element of competition is present. For a more thorough understanding of a theology of sport, see Jeremy R. Treat, "More Than a Game: A Theology of Sport," *Themelios* 40, no. 3 (2015): 392–404.

12. Michael Goheen and Craig Bartholomew help unpack the relationship between one's understanding of the gospel and one's view of sports: "If one embraces a narrow, world-negating view of the gospel, one will have little place for sports and athletic competition. But since the gospel is a gospel about the kingdom of God, sports and competition cannot so easily be jettisoned from a Christian view of things, for these too are gifts of God in creation, to be richly enjoyed with thanksgiving" (Michael Goheen and Craig Bartholomew, *Living at the Crossroads: An Introduction to Christian Worldview* [Grand Rapids: Baker Academic, 2008], 153).

13. The German theologian Jürgen Moltmann once asked whether it is appropriate for Christians to be playing games while war is ravishing the nations, children are starving, and the innocent are being oppressed. It is a weighty question, but I agree with Moltmann when he answers with a resounding yes, because in playing we anticipate a time when there will be no war, a time when sin will not corrupt the goodness in which we are to delight, and a time when our longing for freedom and childlike joy will be satisfied. Jürgen Moltmann, *Theology of Play*, trans. Reinhard Ulrich (New York: Harper & Row, 1972), 2.

14. Buechner, *Wishful Thinking*, 35.

15. The list from the Gospel of Luke, along with this quote by Karris, come from Tim Chester, *A Meal with Jesus: Discovering Grace, Community, and Mission around the Table* (Wheaton, IL: Crossway, 2011), 13.

16. Makoto Fujimura, *Culture Care: Reconnecting with Beauty for Our Common Life* (Downers Grove, IL: IVP, 2017), 16.

17. Bobette Buster, "The Arc of Story Telling," Q, http://qideas.org/videos/the-arc-of-storytelling/.

18. Charles Taylor, *A Secular Age* (Cambridge: Belknap, 2007), 362.

19. Gerald Manly Hopkins, *Hopkins: Poems*, Everyman's Library Pocket Poems (New York: Random House, 1995).

20. Russell Moore, *Onward: Engaging the Culture without Losing the Gospel* (Nashville: B&H, 2015), 28.

21. William Oddie, *Chesterton and the Romance of Orthodoxy: The Making of GKC, 1874–1908* (Oxford: Oxford University Press, 2010), 150.

Chapter 5: Follow Jesus

1. David Brooks, *The Road to Character* (New York: Random House, 2015), 8.

2. All quotes cited in Brooks, 8.

3. Timothy Keller, "The Centrality of the Gospel," gospelinlife.com, http://download.redeemer.com/pdf/learn/resources/Centrality_of_the_Gospel-Keller.pdf.

4. Martin Luther, *St. Paul's Epistle to the Galatians* (Smith, English & Co., 1860), 206.

5. The nineteenth-century Scottish minister Thomas Chalmers helped explain how the gospel does this inside-out work in his sermon "The Expulsive Power of a New Affection." According to Chalmers, ungodly desires for the world cannot merely be displaced; they have to be replaced by the far superior power of the affection of the gospel. In other words, the gospel produces a profound love in the human heart that expels ungodly desires and disordered loves (Thomas Chalmers, *The Expulsive Power of a New Affection* [Minneapolis: Curiosmith, 2012]).

6. Martyn Lloyd-Jones, *Life in the Spirit: In Marriage, Home, and Work—An Exposition of Ephesians 5:18–6:9* (Grand Rapids: Baker, 1979), 11–25.

7. Quoted in Graham A. Cole, *He Who Gives Life: The Doctrine of the Holy Spirit* (Wheaton, IL: Crossway, 2007), 283.

8. For further understanding on the role of habits in shaping our love and life, see James K. A. Smith, *You Are What You Love: The Spiritual Power of Habit* (Grand Rapids: Brazos, 2016).

9. Brooks, *Road to Character*, 264.

10. Theologians throughout church history, beginning with Augustine and Martin Luther, have spoken of sin's tendency to lead humanity to curve in on itself (*incurvatus in se*). This inward bent of sin leads to the attempt to use God as an instrument for our own means rather than worship him as the goal of life.

Chapter 6: Seek Community

1. By "individualistic," I mean a culture that considers and prioritizes the individual before the community. An individualistic culture sees the individual as the basic building block of society, from which everything else, including community, takes its orders. Most cultures throughout world history have been what sociologists call "collectivist" cultures, meaning that the community is the basic building block from which everything else is understood, including individuals. For example, if twenty-first-century Americans are asked, "Who are you?" they will likely respond by sharing their first names and a list of personal accomplishments, such as school, work,

and so on. If persons from a collectivist culture are asked, "Who are you?" they will answer by saying something like, "I'm the son of so-and-so, part of such-and-such tribe, in this particular part of a country." One group sees the world through the lens of individual accomplishments and the other through communal connectedness.

2. Robert D. Putnam, *Bowling Alone: The Collapse and Revival of American Community* (New York: Touchstone, 2001).

3. Sherry Turkle, *Alone Together: Why We Expect More from Technology and Less from Each Other* (New York: Basic Books, 2012).

4. Michael Bird, *Evangelical Theology: A Biblical and Systematic Introduction* (Grand Rapids: Zondervan, 2013), 243.

5. Agbonkhianmeghe Orobator, *Theology Brewed in an African Pot* (Maryknoll, NY: Orbis, 2008), 82.

6. In Matthew 28:18–20 there are four primary verbs: "go," "make disciples," "baptizing," "teaching." One of the verbs is an imperative (a command), and three of the verbs are participles (supporting the primary imperative). Many people assume that "go" is the main thrust of the passage, but actually the one imperative, and therefore the primary charge of the Great Commission, is to "make disciples."

7. Simon Chan, *Grassroots Asian Theology: Thinking the Faith from the Ground Up* (Downers Grove, IL: IVP Academic, 2014), 106.

8. Stanley Hauerwas and William Willimon, *Resident Aliens: Life in the Christian Colony* (Nashville: Abingdon, 1989).

9. Miroslav Volf, *A Public Faith* (Grand Rapids: Brazos, 2013).

10. Ross Douthat, *Bad Religion: How We Became a Nation of Heretics* (New York: Free Press, 2013).

11. Aelred of Rievaulx, *Spiritual Friendship* (Collegeville, MN: Cistercian, 2010), 57.

Chapter 7: Pursue Justice

1. Brian Zisook, "Kendrick Lamar Responded to Our Article about His Fear of God," DJBOOTH, April 28, 2017, http://djbooth.net/news/entry/2017-04-28-kendrick-lamar-god-response (emphasis in original).

2. In fact, if there is no God, there are no grounds for justice at all. German philosopher Friedrich Nietzsche made this case, arguing that if "God is dead," then there is no outside standard for truth or morality. Nietzsche exposed the impossibility of the attempt to uphold Christian morality while doing away with Christian doctrine. Without God we are left to individuals determining their own standards and asserting their own strength. While it's common today for people to say, "What's true for you doesn't have to be true for me," this approach to morality doesn't work in everyday life. Imagine someone saying that to a police officer after breaking the law or to a line of frustrated people at the grocery store after cutting in front of them. Our sense of justice comes from the God of justice.

3. Elaine Scarry, *On Beauty and Being Just*, repr. ed. (Princeton, N.J. Oxford: Princeton University Press, 2001), 91.

4. This vision of God's restorative justice requires his retributive justice. In other words, God's work of redemption entails his work of judgment. For example, to praise God for liberating the captives, we must also praise him for punishing the oppressors (though he certainly redeems oppressors as well). In renewing his creation, God judges and defeats that which seeks to destroy it.

   It is also important, when speaking of justice, to understand the difference between our role and God's role. Romans 12:19 says, "Beloved, never avenge yourselves, but leave it to the wrath of God, for it is written, "Vengeance is mine, I will repay, says the Lord." There is a difference between justice and vengeance. We are not called to seek vengeance; we are called to do justice.

5. Martin Luther King Jr., *Why We Can't Wait* (New York: Signet, 2000), 68.

6. Philosophers have long recognized that there are different versions of justice, which are shaped by one's broader beliefs about life. Aristotle argued that people's views of justice will be determined by what they believe is the telos of life (Aristotle, *Nicomachean Ethics*, trans. Terence Irwin [Indianapolis: Hackett, 1999]). For more recent discussion, see Alasdair MacIntyre, *Whose Justice? Which Rationality?* (Notre Dame, IN: University

of Notre Dame Press, 1989); Michael J. Sandel, *Justice: What's the Right Thing to Do?* (New York: Farrar, Straus and Giroux, 2010).

7. Aristotle, *Nicomachean Ethics.*

8. John Perkins, Twitter, February 13, 2017, https://twitter.com/JohnMPerkins/status/831348073939030016.

9. Nicholas Wolterstorff, philosopher and former professor at Yale, argues that a secular grounding of human rights is impossible (*Justice: Rights and Wrongs* [Princeton, NJ: Princeton University Press, 2010], 323–41).

10. Martin Luther King Jr., in a sermon on the rich young ruler, spoke of "the interrelated structure of reality." King said, "All men are caught in an inescapable network of mutuality, tied in a single garment of destiny. Whatever affects one directly affects all indirectly. I can never be what I ought to be until you are what you ought to be, and you can never be what you ought to be until I am what I ought to be" (Martin Luther King Jr., *Strength to Love* [Minneapolis: Fortress, 2010], 69).

11. A "needs-based" approach is built on the assumption that some are needy and some have solutions. This creates a false divide that ends up reinforcing the problem while allowing the helpers to feel better about themselves and their service. A "dignity-driven" approach puts us all on the same playing field and seeks to affirm dignity, help people use their own resources, and empower them for sustainable health.

    Martin Luther King Jr. modeled a dignity-driven approach. In a sermon on the story of the good Samaritan, King says, "The real tragedy . . . is that we see people as entities or merely as things. Too seldom do we see people in their true humanness. A spiritual myopia limits our vision to external accidents. We see men as Jews or Gentiles, Catholics or Protestants, Chinese or American, Negroes or whites. We fail to think of them as fellow human beings made from the same basic stuff as we, molded in the same divine image. . . . The good neighbor looks beyond the external accidents and discerns those inner qualities that make all men human" (King, *Strength to Love*, 24–25).

12. While such a dichotomy makes no sense according to Scripture, a quick historical sketch will explain how we ended up in such a situation. In the 1930s, with a great economic depression setting in, many churches in (liberal) mainline traditions began emphasizing the biblical call to care for the poor and confront systemic injustice. Sadly, many of these same churches did so at the expense of traditional biblical doctrines, such as the inerrancy of Scripture, the sinfulness of humanity, and substitutionary atonement.

"The gospel"—so the story went—"is not so much about grace for your sins; it's about what we can do to show God's love to others." The problem was not merely that the gospel was downplayed by pressing needs, but that it was redefined as something we do for God, rather than what he has done for us. Furthermore, this "social gospel" movement often appealed to the kingdom as the framework for what they were doing. "Kingdom" language increasingly became associated primarily with serving the poor and helping the hurting while it was disassociated from what God has done for us in the life, death, and resurrection of Jesus. The kingdom was reduced to human efforts to make the world a better place.

13. Timothy Keller, *Generous Justice: How God's Grace Makes Us Just* (New York: Riverhead, 2012), 93–94.

14. Dietrich Bonhoeffer, *Life Together* (San Francisco: HarperSanFrancisco, 1993), 97.

15. Richard Bauckham, *Bible and Mission: Christian Witness in a Postmodern World* (Grand Rapids: Baker, 2003), 9.

16. David McClendon, "Sub-Saharan Africa Will Be Home to Growing Shares of the World's Christians and Muslims," Pew Research Center, April 19, 2017, www.pewresearch.org/fact-tank/2017/04/19/sub-saharan-africa-will-be-home-to-growing-shares-of-the-worlds-christians-and-muslims/.

17. Gordon-Conwell Resources, "Global Christianity: A Look at the Status of Christianity in 2018," www.gordonconwell.edu/ockenga/research/Resources-and-Downloads.cfm.

18. Athanasius, *On the Incarnation* (Crestwood, NY: St. Vladimir's Seminary Press, 2002), 55.

19. Bob Smietana, "Sunday Morning in America Still Segregated—and That's OK with Worshipers," LifeWay Research, January 15, 2015, https://lifewayresearch.com/2015/01/15/Sunday-morning-in-america-still-segregated-and-thats-ok-with-worshipers/.

20. Much could be said about Christianity's past with racism, but I will offer three brief points: (1) The church has clearly been complicit in racism. Many of our most influential theologians were explicitly racist, some even holding slaves. Beyond individuals, some churches, denominations, and Christian institutions have held and advanced explicitly racist policies. (2) The church has also been at the forefront of fighting against racism and for racial equity. Individuals, churches, denominations, and Christian institutions have led the way globally in fighting racism based on the biblical teaching that all are made in the image of God. (3) When the church has supported racism, it has not been true to its Lord and his calling on his people. When the church has sought equality among races, it has reflected the heart of God. In other words, the failure of Christians (and many so-called Christians) is not a reflection of Christ and his heart for the nations.

21. Cesar Chavez, *An Organizer's Tale: Speeches* (New York: Penguin, 2008), 352.

22. John Perkins, "A Letter to the Seattle Pacific University Community," *Response* 27.4 (2004). The letter can also be read online: https://spu.edu/depts/uc/response/autumn2k4/letterfromJohn.asp.

Chapter 8: Sons and Daughters

1. John Wikstrom, *Finding Benjaman*, 2012, https://vimeo.com/34589969.

2. For an excellent overview of the biblical theme of God's people as a "royal priesthood," see Uche Anizor and Hank Voss, *Representing Christ: A Vision for the Priesthood of All Believers* (Downers Grove, IL: IVP Academic, 2016).

3. Quoted in Levi Tucker, *Lectures on the Nature and Dangerous Tendency of Modern Infidelity* (Cleveland: Francis B. Penniman, 1837), 141.

4. The doctrine of union with Christ has been revolutionary for me personally. Not only does union with Christ bring together so many theological concepts (for example, justification and sanctification), but it also helps bring them to bear on daily life in a personal and practical way.

   I was first struck by the importance of union with Christ from reading John Calvin's *Institutes of the Christian Religion*. After expounding the glory of God's character and all the benefits of salvation in Christ for hundreds of pages, Calvin then says, "How do we receive those benefits which the Father bestowed on his only-begotten Son . . . ? First, we must understand that as long as Christ remains outside of us, and we are separated from him, all that he has suffered and done for the salvation of the human race remains useless and of no value for us. . . . The Holy Spirit is the bond by which Christ effectually unites us to himself" (John Calvin, *Institutes of the Christian Religion*, ed. John McNeill, trans. Ford Lewis Battles [Louisville: Westminster John Knox, 2006], 3.1.1). In other words, apart from Christ, we're separated from the riches of God's grace. But in Christ we have every spiritual blessing. Everything hinges on union with Christ.

Chapter 9: Sojourners and Exiles

1. "America's Changing Religious Landscape," Pew Research Center, May 12, 2015, www.pewforum.org/2015/05/12/americas-changing-religious-landscape/.
2. Charles Taylor's *A Secular Age* (Cambridge: Belknap, 2007) represents a vast amount of scholarship disproving the "secularization thesis." Taylor demonstrates that when one attempts to subtract religion from society, it does not leave a neutral, secular space but rather is replaced with other faith-based beliefs and values.
3. For a helpful and concise overview of how the world is becoming more religious, see Timothy Keller, "Isn't Religion Going Away?" in *Making Sense of God: An Invitation to the Skeptical* (New York: Viking, 2016), ch. 1.

4. Daniel Meyer, *Witness Essentials: Evangelism That Makes Disciples* (Downers Grove, Ill: InterVarsity, 2012), 33.

5. Wes Granberg-Michaelson, "Think Christianity Is Dying? No, Christianity Is Shifting Dramatically," *Washington Post*, May 20, 2015, www.washingtonpost.com/news/acts-of-faith/ wp/2015/05/20/think-christianity-is-dying-no-christianity-is -shifting-dramatically/?utm_term=.4c1847f10aab.

6. "Appendix C: Methodology for China," Pew Research Center, December 19, 2011, http://www.pewresearch.org/wp-content/ uploads/sites/7/2011/12/ChristianityAppendixC.pdf.

7. Granberg-Michaelson, "Think Christianity Is Dying?"

8. "Global Christianity: A Report on the Size and Distribution of the World's Christian Population," Pew Research Center, December 2011, www.pewforum.org/files/2011/12/Christianity -fullreport-web.pdf.

9. Based on the research of Operation World, "Of the world's approximately 6,900 languages, 4,765 have at least one of the following: Bible portions, the Jesus Film, Christian radio, or Gospel recordings." "Mission Stats: The Current State of the World," Traveling Team, www.thetravelingteam.org/stats/.

10. "Religious Landscape Study," Pew Research Center, www.pew forum.org/religious-landscape-study/; and "Attendance at Religious Services," Pew Research Center, www.pewforum.org/ religious-landscape-study/attendance-at-religious-services/ #demographic-information.

11. Frederick Douglass, *Narrative of the Life of Frederick Douglass, An American Slave: Written by Himself* (New Haven: Yale University Press, 2001), 81.

12. Miroslav Volf, *A Public Faith* (Grand Rapids: Brazos, 2013), 93. See also James Davidson Hunter's idea of "faithful presence" in *To Change the World: The Irony, Tragedy, and Possibility of Christianity in the Late Modern World* (New York: Oxford University Press, 2010).

13. J. Todd Billings helpfully argues that union with Christ is a more fruitful framework for ministry than incarnational ministry. While much is to be commended in an "incarnational

ministry" approach (e.g., presence in the city), there are two problems: (1) the incarnation of Christ is a unique event in history that cannot be replicated by humanity, and (2) it is a framework that emphasizes imitation more than participation. A better way forward is to think of ministry as union with Christ. Jesus continues his mission, and we get to participate in ministry inasmuch as we are united to Christ (J. Todd Billings, *Union with Christ: Reframing Theology and Ministry for the Church* [Grand Rapids: Baker Academic, 2011], 123–66).

14. See John D. Inazu, *Confident Pluralism: Surviving and Thriving through Deep Difference* (Chicago: University of Chicago Press, 2016).

15. Volf, *Public Faith*, xv.

16. Angukali Rotokha, "Daniel," in *South Asia Bible Commentary*, ed. Brian Wintle (Grand Rapids: Zondervan, 2015), 1084.

Chapter 10: Saints and Sinners

1. John Newton, "Unhappy Instance of Conformity to the World," *The Christian Spectator* 3 (1821): 186.

2. Joel Stein, "A Little Bit of Heaven on Earth," *Los Angeles Times*, December 21, 2007, http://articles.latimes.com/2007/dec/21/news/OE-STEIN21.

3. A key aspect of the theme of God dwelling in the temple is the holy of holies. This was a small room in the temple and was the strongest manifestation of God's presence on earth. Only the high priest could enter this place once a year. When Jesus died on the cross, the veil of the holy of holies was torn down the middle, symbolizing that God's presence had been unleashed and was now available to all by grace. In Revelation 21, where the dimensions of the New Jerusalem coming from heaven are given, the dimensions are in proportion to those of the holy of holies in the original Jerusalem temple. In the new creation, the holy of holies is everywhere, and God's presence will be seen and experienced in its fullness.

4. Scholars call this "inaugurated eschatology," meaning that the end times (eschatology) have already begun (or been inaugurated) in the middle of history. This is a helpful correction to

overrealized eschatology (expecting the fullness of the king-dom today) and to underrealized eschatology (waiting for all of the kingdom's power in the future).
5. In a pivotal moment in *The Return of the King*, Sam asks Gandalf, "Is everything sad going to come untrue?" (J. R. R. Tolkien, *The Return of the King* [New York: Del Rey, 1986], 246).